TRACING YOUR POLICE ANCESTORS

Other Titles in Pen & Sword Family History

TRACING YOUR POLICE ANCESTORS

Stephen Wade

Pen & Sword
FAMILY HISTORY

Essex County
Council Libraries

First published in Great Britain in 2009 by
PEN & SWORD FAMILY HISTORY
an imprint of
Pen & Sword Books Ltd
47 Church Street
Barnsley
South Yorkshire
S70 2AS

ISBN 978 1 84415 878 2

A CIP catalogue record for this book is
available from the British Library.

Typeset in Palatino and Optima by
Phoenix Typesetting, Auldgirth, Dumfriesshire

Printed and bound in England by
CPI UK

Pen & Sword Books Ltd incorporates the Imprints of
Pen & Sword Aviation, Pen & Sword Maritime, Pen & Sword Military, Wharncliffe Local
History, Pen & Sword Select, Pen & Sword Military Classics and Leo Cooper.

For a complete list of Pen & Sword titles please contact
PEN & SWORD BOOKS LIMITED
47 Church Street, Barnsley, South Yorkshire, S70 2AS, England
E-mail: enquiries@pen-and-sword.co.uk
Website: www.pen-and-sword.co.uk

CONTENTS

ACKNOWLEDGEMENTS

Thanks are due to Roger Appleby of the City of London Police Museum; Crispin Williams of Shaw & Sons, for permission to use the image of the *Police and Constabulary Almanac*; Lincolnshire Archives Illustrations Index, and the Essex Police Museum for the images as credited. The picture of the police ambulance is reprinted by permission of the Greater Manchester Police Museum. Staff at the East Riding Archives and at Lincolnshire Archives were most helpful in guiding me to the relevant material, and equally the staff at the London Metropolitan Archives took the time to answer queries. Conversations with retired officers proved useful also, as a certain element of oral history is clearly of great assistance in an enterprise such as this.

As always in writing history, there are pathfinders to thank as well, in this case Les Waters and his Police History Society monograph. This was the first publication that attempted to bring together the various strands of material involved in this research. Other progress is down to members of the Police History Society and individuals such as Fred Feather, Dr John Bond and Paul Williams, as mentioned in the Bibliography.

A TIME-LINE
FOR POLICE HISTORY

1750s   Henry and John Fielding active as London magistrates. Bow Street Runners formed, 'originally consisting of the only six of the eighty Constables in Westminster not on the take' (Oliver Cyriax, *The Penguin Encyclopaedia of Crime*).

1796   Publication of Patrick Colquhoun's book, *A Treatise on the Police of the Metropolis*.

1829   Metropolitan Police Act. Robert Peel forms the first professional force, for London.

1835   Municipal Corporations Act. This brought about the formation of Watch Committees, created by boroughs.

1836   The Royal Irish Constabulary formed by Thomas Drummond.

1837   John Kent, the first black police constable, joins the Carlisle force.

1839   The formation of the City of London Police.

1842   The first detective force formed.

1839   The County Police Act. This gave boroughs the option of forming a constabulary if the justices wanted to levy a rate for that purpose.

1856   The County and Borough Police Act. This made it compulsory for all counties in England and Wales to establish police forces.

1874   The Criminal Investigation Department established.

1890   Police Pensions Act. Under this Act, receipt of a pension after 25 years' service became a right.

1911   Captain Horwood becomes the Chief Officer of the Eastern Railway Police. (He later became Commissioner of the Metropolitan Police.)

1915	The first woman police officer appointed (Edith Smith, Grantham).
1917	The first policewomen are sworn in for service in the Transport Police for the North-Eastern Railway.
1918–1919	Police strikes in London and Liverpool.
1920	The Police Pensions Act. This defined the age limit for each rank at retirement.
1920	Creation of the Palestine Police Force.
1922	The Royal Ulster Constabulary is formed.
1924	The Metropolitan Police start to relinquish dockyard duties.
1924	Ada Atherton starts work at Waterloo as a female detective for the Transport Police.
1930	A sign of changing times: large numbers of officers begin traffic patrol work.
1932	The beat system is abolished by Lord Trenchard.
1933	The Metropolitan Police College at Hendon is opened.
1934	The Metropolitan Forensic Laboratory is opened.
1941	PC William Brereton is awarded the British Empire Medal for gallant conduct. During an air raid on a goods depot in South London he saved the life of PC Rowing inside a burning building.
1948	The British Mandate for Palestine ends: the Palestine Police Force is disbanded.
1955	The Central Traffic Squad is formed: a hundred men are involved in this.
1963–1975	Gradual rationalisation of forces and disbandment of many smaller constabularies.
1965	The Special Patrol Group is formed: 100 officers arrest 396 people in the first year of work.
1966	Norwell Roberts joins the Met. as the first black police officer in that force. (He was to receive the Queen's Police Medal in 1996.)

INTRODUCTION

Survey of Sources

The history of the professional police force in Britain presents the historian of law and crime with a very full and detailed record. For the family historian, however, that is not the case. It is a simple matter to find out what the various police archives contain, but problems arise from the fact that many of the useful records are not where logic might dictate they should be found. Many police staff records, or even documents that contain information about constables, are either simply not available or perhaps dispersed across a range of sources.

But there is some good news. With perseverance, a determination to work through a number of ephemeral records and some detective work, most police ancestors can be found, although the information that is actually found is variable in the extreme. The root cause of this difficulty is that the original county and borough forces, formed between 1838 and 1856, were steadily changed, reorganised and rationalised as police organisation progressed. Therefore some records dating to a period when a particular constabulary was in existence may have been abandoned when a new force was formed. There was also a most haphazard approach to the preservation of police records and at times very little effort was put in to the concept of creating an ordered and systematic archive in some forces.

The City of London Police force, for instance, has its own museum at the Wood Street station; there in two small rooms a large amount of materials is preserved and there are extensive records of staff. But other related materials and documents are also to be found at the London Metropolitan Archives and also at the Museum of London. The family detective therefore has to travel and to be persistent in the search for an ancestor, particularly if more than the bare facts of date of service and rank are needed. Sources are therefore plentiful but disparate and inconsistent. Fortunately, the Police History Society has published a book containing the basic statistics of all the police forces since Peel's first

Police Act of 1829. This is Martin Stallion and David S. Wall's *The British Police: Police Forces and Chief Officers 1829–2000*. This invaluable reference work gives the reader the dates of each force's existence, its initial and final manpower and its chief officers. For instance, there we will discover that the Bristol Constabulary was formed in 1836, with an initial strength of around 230 men, and was dissolved in 1974 when it became part of Avon and Somerset. The first chief officer was Joseph Bishop and the last one was George Twist.

Referring to Stallion and Wall will give the historian the basic facts of the existence of the force the ancestor was in: that is a useful starting-point and in most cases leads to the relevant records. Subsequently, the historian has to be prepared to do some digging around limited documents, looking for the ancestor's involvement in certain crimes or any other recorded events.

The Guide to Archives: Police History Society

Available sources range from charge books to memoirs, so it is essential that some kind of general listing of holdings be consulted, and the only one in existence is now online as part of the Open University website. This guide to the archives was originally compiled by Ian Bridgeman and Martin Stallion, and then enlarged by Clive Emsley. As the authors wrote in their preface to this extensive archive in 1989, 'The documents listed below contain a wealth of information on the ordering and control of urban and rural life from the mid-nineteenth century, on the supervision of strikes and protest marches, the treatment of aliens, the impact of twentieth-century total war . . .'. The guide consists of an alphabetical index based on the current names of the police forces, and it includes any material not deposited at the National Archives, including items from the Metropolitan Police and the British Transport Police. The ordering is as follows:

1. Administrative items such as reports

2. Crime registers, prisoners and photo albums

3. Force instructions: general orders, memoranda, etc.

4. Station journals, occurrence books, 'Lost and Found', and pocket books/beat books

5. Personnel: registers, rolls and discipline records

6. Watch Committee and Standing Joint Committee: minute books/chief constables' reports

7. Miscellaneous: special constables, etc.

Clearly, for the present purposes, section 5 is the most relevant. For instance, if one looks under the West Yorkshire Police section, locating the Bradford City Police (abolished in 1974), there are many items that could be useful in a family history search:

1. Examination of candidates register for 1897–1911

2. Register of officers and constables, 1918–1945

3. Defaulters' book for 1883–1896

4. Chief constables' report books for 1902–1974

5. Report on insubordinate language – Sidney Chamberlain

The choice of Bradford was merely random but it illustrates the types of document that may be found. If your ancestor was a constable, then in that particular archive for his period in office, there may only be a simple record of his dates and perhaps a comment when he passed an examination. If he misbehaved or was insubordinate then you would have something else. In other words, as with much family history, the narrative we compile is amplified when there are events happening outside the routine, which for the police could be anything from a major riot to an obscenity spoken while on duty.

We will return to an examination of this guide later (see p. 132).

Specialist Groups

The following organisations are all listed at the back of this book, with addresses, websites and other information.

The **Police History Society** is not primarily concerned with family history, but there is no doubt that its publications have an important role to play in the necessary detective work of tracing police ancestors. The journal is published annually and offers ample evidence that society members have considerable knowledge in such areas as police duty and conditions of service in years gone by, and also have specific research interests in areas that naturally bring to light names, events and places that may help to amplify information on a person at the centre of a family historian's research.

The **Imperial War Museum** has material on the work done by women police, including such items as letters, diaries and photographs relating to women who served in the Women's Police Service in the First World War. On the subject of women police, the **National Police Library** in Hampshire has a substantial library on the topic; the books are primarily for serving employees in the police but they may be accessed using the inter-library loan service.

The **British Transport Police History Society** has a useful website at www.btp.police.com. This provides a very handy chronology of the force and other materials. Since the publication in 1961 of J.R. Whitbread's book *The Railway Policeman* (*see* Bibliography) there has been an acceleration of interest in this area of police work, partly because of the continuing interest in railway history as a hobby generally. Silver Link Publishing, a specialist publisher of railway books, has included a case book of railway crime in its lists, and these kinds of resources fill out the reports in newspapers which so often enhance a biographical enquiry.

The **Police Officers Roll of Honour Trust** is based in Preston and can help with information on officers from the past who have been notable for their special actions and distinctions. This, together with the resources held by Paul Williams at Murderfiles.com (see Bibliography), may provide a substantial resource relating to any ancestors who were distinguished in the course of duty, particularly if they lost their lives in acts of bravery and sacrifice. In The Times for 3 September 1830, within a year of the establishment of the new police, a correspondent wrote, 'In conclusion, I beg you to receive 10s for the use of the widow and family of poor Long, the policeman who appears to have fallen in the zealous exercise of his duties.' PC Long had been murdered in Holborn, the first fatality in the ranks of the new 'Peelers.' Once again, exceptional events provide a new narrative for the historian.

The **European Centre for the Study of Policing** is linked to the International Centre for Comparative Criminological Research, and its publications often add to local police studies. Recently published articles have touched on various topics, such as police archives and the Sheffield Police 1832–40, while a book by Chris Williams, *Giving the Past a Future*, is concerned with preserving records of the criminal justice system.

There is also the **Bibliography of British Police History**, the database being at www.open.ac.uk/Arts/policebiblio/search.cfm. This is being enlarged all the time, and includes every conceivable topic within police studies.

Museums

As already mentioned, the Open University holdings, which include the former Police History Society listings of regional archives, is at the centre of police family history research. In addition, another fundamental resource is at Access to Archives, known as A2A. Here, the family historian will find a list of archive materials in all the major educational institutions in the United Kingdom. For instance, an A2A search for Lincolnshire Archives, using the search word 'police', leads to these items:

> Lincolnshire County Committee 1889–1975
>
> Lincolnshire Gaol Sessions
>
> Minute Book 1916–1922
>
> Papers from private collections

Within these, for example, there are notes from the Petty Sessional Division on rural police and there the superintendents for each area of Lincolnshire in 1857 are given, such as 'George Hardcastle. Pay £120 with horse' and 'George Sharpe, in charge of a lock-up, Sleaford. Salary £120 including the keeping of a horse.' There is also a personal file of newspaper cuttings kept by a constable, who diligently collected reports on all the cases in which he was involved. This cache illustrates the sheer diversity of materials available in police archives.

Principal police museums include the Ripon Museum Trust, which has a massive collection with plenty of resources relating to personnel; it also has a heritage site museum, including a police building, gaol and courthouse. Their listing on A2A gives a representative summary of what material in police records is of particular interest when trying to trace a police officer in your family from the past. For instance, Ripon has 'expenses for Robert Andrews at Whitby court', 'eight warning notices for attendance at Assize and quarter sessions for a police constable 1943–1952' and 'a cuttings file involving PC Redgwick'. Once again, we have to notice the special usefulness of ephemera in this area of family history.

Not all police museums are open to the public, and so it will sometimes be necessary to make appointments to visit. The main ones are in Cumbria, Essex, Greater Manchester, Kent, South Wales (Bridgend), Tetbury, Thames Valley and Winchcombe. Essex provides particularly useful materials on police history, and their stories provide points of departure for enquiries into such areas of police history as regional detective work, medals and awards, disciplinary actions, dog units and marine policing.

The benefits of visiting a police museum for family historians are mainly concerned with gaining a quick recognition of what the documents, everyday materials and professional artefacts are like. But at some of these museums there will also be records of staff, as at Thames Valley, where there are lists of officers who served in Reading Borough and in Oxfordshire. Chapter 11 provides more details on the most prominent museums.

Finally, there is the resource provided by Fred Feather at **Research into Family and Police History**, based in Essex (*see* Bibliography and websites). Fred Feather is a contributor to *The Family and Local History Handbook* and other publications. He was formerly the curator of the Essex Police Museum.

When all else fails in the course of a search, there is the website Roots Web, and there researchers will find a special section for police ancestry queries. Once again, Fred Feather will often reply, such is his knowledge and experience, along with other Police History Society members and museum curators.

Chapter 1

A SHORT HISTORY OF THE POLICE

Local Constables

The development of a professional police force in Britain presents us with a story of local provision, steps taken in response to urgent need and ad hoc measures taken in time of such events as political revolt or mass riot. The system before the Victorian reforms was one stretching back to the thirteenth century, when the parish constable was gradually established from the Saxon 'Tithingmen'; it was a post of great responsibility. Of course, there had been a county sheriff (a 'shire-reeve' in earlier times) with broader remits for the whole county, but in terms of each community the parish constable was at the centre of local police work. Backing him were the justices of the peace, men doing judicial work for no payment.

In the seventeenth century we can trace the emergence of 'watch and ward'. This meant that so-called 'charlies' (named thus because they emerged in the reign of Charles II) became the people responsible for day and night watch shifts. Usually carrying a lantern, they walked a specific area, and sometimes also stood at major thoroughfares, sometimes in a box. The local parish constables and the watch and ward system were never a universally disciplined and organised concept. If we look at some records of the West Riding Quarter Sessions for 1638, for instance, we gain an insight into where the constable stood with regard to the local justice process. They were often named, so the family historian will find these documents an enticing prospect if their enquiries go back beyond the Victorian period. This is a typical entry made at those sessions:

> Constable's Accounts. Whereas John Fowler and Samuel Walton, late constables of Halifax, have not made any account of the monyes they received last yeare upon their constables layes [levy or rate] within the towne of Halifax, ORDERED that they shall accounte before Mr Nathaniell Waterhowse, Mr Robert Exley and the present constable before May 1 next.

The notion of a constable originates in the folk moot system, and the word derives from the Latin *comes stabuli*, 'master of the horse'. The constables were usually chosen from the members of the Vestry Committee, and of course officers assigned to the work had to keep on with their own trades and businesses as well as carrying out their police work. Until lock-ups were established, the parish constable would some-times have to keep prisoners secure in his own dwelling. In the Lincolnshire village of Hibaldstow stands a row of four seventeenth-century cottages, one of which is known to have been the former constable's house. It had a makeshift gaol within its walls.

Each parish would have between four and six parish constables, but they wore no distinctive uniform. A photograph exists of Mr Gater Potter, who was the last parish constable of Abbotskerswell, Newton Abbot. The picture was taken in 1857, but Mr Potter had been a constable

The Cranford lock-up at Bath Road, Middlesex.
(Author)

since 1829. Until the 1856 Act discussed below, there would have been many such figures around the country, seeing to prisoners, following up requests for help, settling disputes and reporting to magistrates.

Watch and Ward

A useful way to gain an insight into the workings of the Vestry Committee is to examine a case study. In Richmond the Teddington Association for Proper Persons met in the Vestry Room in 1822 to organise their two police 'patroles' (a watch and ward beat system). This followed the precedent of the London night patroles which had emerged from the work of John Colquhoun before Peel's Act. It cost Richmond around £50 to maintain this vigilant group in the streets at night. Twickenham Reference Library has detailed material on this Vestry work and on the constables, and these minutes open up their work for the modern historian in interesting detail:

> Richard William Cook and John Harris having been proposed as proper persons to act as Patroles – Resolved – That they be appointed accordingly, and paid at the rate of one guinea per week each, and that they be provided with proper arms at the expense of this Association. It is extremely desirable that the said persons should be appointed Constables.
> Resolved – That an application be made to Mr Sergeant Marshall, requesting that he will swear them in accordingly . . .

The Watch in Richmond was superseded by the new V Division of the Metropolitan Police in January 1840 and the former watch-houses were taken over as police stations. For the family historian, the accounts and minutes of the Vestry subscription fund provide names, of both police officers and villains, such as: 'Nov. to the parish constable and his assistants of Kingston who apprehended Brown . . . £3 3s.

The New Police

The Metropolitan Police was officially formed on 29 September 1829. It had existed in statute law since July, but the first men did not go out on patrol until the end of September. Even before that date there had been extensive criticism of the idea and of the men being recruited. Referring to the new guidebook produced for officers, the *Sunday Times* of 27 September thundered:

> If the recruits can understand, or even read through it in a year, they will certainly be very different from their thief-taking predecessors. However, we suppose this may be calculated upon, for we have heard so much of the care taken by the commissioners to guard against enlisting any but proper and accomplished persons . . . that it is a relief to find . . . that university honours are not required to prove the fitness of the individuals applying for a situation which is to bring them in 3s. per diem.

This kind of satirical carping was much in evidence at the time, but Robert Peel had chosen well in selecting the two commissioners who would lead and create the new police force. They were Sir Charles Rowan, a veteran of the Napoleonic Wars and a former justice operating in Ireland, and the young lawyer Richard Mayne. Peel had been Home Secretary in 1822 and later became Prime Minister, putting reform of the criminal justice system high on his agenda. He had earlier passed legislation concerning gaol reforms and he next turned his attention to the need for a professional police force, after theoretical work by Colquhoun, who had published *A Treatise on the Police of the Metropolis* in 1796, had raised and dealt with the major policing issues in the context of increased crime, frequent riots in the streets and the effects of the wars with France.

The English people were suspicious of the idea of professional police even while Peel was at work processing his Bill. After all, the government's repression of working-class radicalism in the first decades of the nineteenth century had been savage, and *agents provocateurs* had been used to locate the leaders of dissent. This led to the common usage of the phrase 'police spies' and suspicion increased. In addition, local problems of disorder had been met with military action, too: the local militias were regularly called out to deal with open protests and demonstrations, most infamously in the Peterloo Massacre of 1819 in Manchester, when a peaceful crowd that had gathered to hear Henry Hunt speak in support of parliamentary reform was attacked by yeomanry and hussars. Eleven people were killed and some five hundred wounded.

But the Bill went through and the new police appeared on the streets of London. The commissioners had rooms at the Home Office and then

A

TREATISE

ON THE

POLICE OF THE METROPOLIS;

CONTAINING A DETAIL OF THE

VARIOUS CRIMES AND MISDEMEANORS

By which Public and Private Property and Security are, at present, injured and endangered:

AND

SUGGESTING REMEDIES

FOR THEIR

PREVENTION.

THE SEVENTH EDITION, CORRECTED AND CONSIDERABLY ENLARGED.

BY P. COLQUHOUN, LL.D.

Acting as a Magistrate for the Counties of Middlesex, Surry, Kent, and Essex.—For the City and Liberty of Westminster, and for the Liberty of the Tower of London.

Meminerint legum conditores, illas ad proximum hunc finem accommodare; Scelera videlicet arcenda, refrænandaque vitia ac morum pravitatem.

Judices pariter leges illas cum vigore, æquitate, integritate, publicæque utilitatis amore curent exequi; ut justitia et virtus omnes societatis ordines prevadant. Industriaque simul et Temperantia inertiæ locum assumant et prodigalitatis.

LONDON:

PRINTED FOR J. MAWMAN, CADELL AND DAVIES, R. FAULDER, CLARKE AND SONS, LONGMAN, HURST, REES AND ORME, VERNOR, HOOD, AND SHARPE, H. D. SYMONDS, LACKINGTON, ALLEN, AND CO. SCATCHERD AND LETTERMAN, R. LEA, B. CROSBY AND CO. WYNNE AND SON, R. PHENEY, BLACKS AND PARRY, J. ASPERNE; AND WILSON AND SPENCE, YORK.

1806.

The title page of P. Colquhoun's Treatise on the Police of the Metropolis. (Author) at 4 Whitehall Place, an area always known as 'Scotland', and from this emerged 'Scotland Yard'. (As an aside, the architect Sir Christopher Wren had once kept materials in the yard there.) The new force was split into seventeen Divisions, defined by letters of the alphabet, and two-thirds of the officers were on duty at night, for obvious reasons. They worked on beats from 9 pm to 6 am and had to move at 2½ miles an hour. Each Division had a superintendent, who had to report every morning to Scotland Yard. The total strength of the force in May 1830 was just over three thousand men.

Following the 1829 Act, other measures were soon taken to try to

Sir Charles Rowan, one of the first Metropolitan Police commissioners.
(Laura Carter)

streamline matters in terms of organisation and effectiveness. Resources were limited: there were, for example, only 46 horses on the force, and these were hired contractually. In everyday matters of equipment and uniform, the clothing supplied to the new officers included a greatcoat, a blue coat, two pairs of trousers, a hat and cape, and boots. For weapons, officers were issued with cutlasses, based on the type used by the navy. A Metropolitan Police Order written in 1832 stated that 'The police constable is to be given to understand distinctly that the sword is put into his hand merely as a defensive weapon'. As time went on, more thought was given to defence against attacks, including the wearing of thick collars to prevent them being strangled from behind.

The key statement regarding responsibility and behaviour was given in an order of 1830 in which the commissioners stated: 'the police . . . should do their duty with every possible moderation and forbearance, and they should not furnish complaint against themselves by any misconduct'. In fact, a high proportion of men left the force or were sacked, usually through drunkenness, in the early years.

Police Reform in the Victorian Period

From 1829 to 1856 there was slow progress towards the creation of a professional police force across the country, with specific legislation being made on the way. The first step came in 1833 with the Lighting and Watching Police Act. The commissioners for the Municipal Corporations enquired into the constabulary availability and efficiency in the boroughs. The Lighting and Watching Act made it possible for men of substance in the towns to become inspectors, enabling them to appoint police staff. If the traditional system of parish constables was considered to be inadequate, then this could be done. At a time when the impact of the Industrial Revolution was causing radical changes in population location, with people flocking to the towns to find work in the new industries, urban problems soon arose and the old ways were often found to be falling short when it came to dealing with offences.

Occasionally, if there was a complaint regarding the burden of paying rates for the measures taken under this act, there will be a record of it with names attached. Therefore it is worth noting that in research the keywords 'lighting' and 'watching' may lead to the identification of constables. That was certainly the case in the monograph based on Horncastle in Lincolnshire by B.J. Davey (*see* Bibliography).

In 1836 another result of the 1835 Municipal Corporations Act brought about more police measures. Some new borough police forces were formed, with the Watch Committees directing them. Because there was some method of control and appointment here, the minute books of the various watch committees may contain names of officers. But it was the 1839 County Police Act that really reformed the police. This act appointed Constabulary Commissioners, and the idea was that rural and provincial forces would be formed on the 'New Police' London system. The report written for this details the procedures established, and local case studies often provide examples of how it worked.

For instance, Roger Swift's monograph on York, *Police Reform in Early Victorian York 1835–1856* (*see* Bibliography), gives an account of the opposition to the new legislation and gives sound economic reasons for that resistance. He also explains the relationship of the Watch Committee to

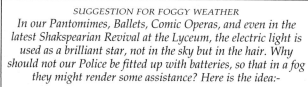

SUGGESTION FOR FOGGY WEATHER
In our Pantomimes, Ballets, Comic Operas, and even in the latest Shakspearian Revival at the Lyceum, the electric light is used as a brilliant star, not in the sky but in the hair. Why should not our Police be fitted up with batteries, so that in a fog they might render some assistance? Here is the idea:-

Punch cartoon dealing with early police work.
(Author)

the new force, as in the measures taken for special duties, pointing out that such duties carried an allowance of 10s 6d per day for a superintendent and 5s for a constable.

The 1839 act opened up the adoption of new measures, such as the introduction of special constables by justices at the Quarter Sessions, paid for by means of levying a rate. It was done in a climate of anxiety and fear on the part of the authorities, as the massive Chartist movement for franchise reform was escalating and special constables, along with militia, were being used where possible. But in local terms, special constables were regarded as traitors and spies, and it proved difficult to recruit them in many areas. The areas that did adopt the new measures provide useful historical documentation, and the materials available give the researcher information on what actually happened at the local level.

In 1842 the passing of the Parish Constables Act opened up the possibility of installing paid constables who would work in a lock-up system; this was a stop-gap measure to deal with rural crime and to help make the criminal justice system work, with more options in terms of petty crime and minor offences. This notice, issued by the magistrates in North Yorkshire, makes the measures clear:

> [That] a lock-up house should be provided and built at Northallerton in the said Riding and that the sum of £230 should be granted out of the funds of the Riding for that purpose . . . and the Right Reverend Father in God Charles Thomas, Lord Bishop of Durham, lord of this manor hath agreed to give and grant with consent . . . the plot or piece of waste land . . . for the site of a lock-up house at Northallerton . . .

A police sergeant handcuffed to a woman prisoner. (Reproduced by courtesy of Lincolnshire County Council; from the local studies collection)

Clearly the work of rural policemen was very hard indeed, and it is no surprise that in the records we find references to dismissals and disciplinary proceedings as well as general appointments. Here, once again, the unusual rather than the routine gives rise to records and actual names in the local police narratives.

The most significant legislation came in 1856 with the County and Borough Police Act. After the report of a Select Committee on Police in 1853, it was made compulsory for county forces to be created and for some amalgamations to be effected. To supervise this, special officers were created, known as Her Majesty's Inspectors of Constabulary. The report of 1853 had stressed the vagrancy problem, which was considered to be a major cause of crime, and in the larger rural counties we can see the varying implementations of this Act taking that into consideration. In Lincolnshire, for example, the Chief Constable's report on the Lincolnshire Constabulary given to the Joint Police Committee in 1857 lists the strength of the force: Lindsey had 7 superintendents and 43 constables; Kesteven had 1 superintendent and 20 constables, and Holland had 1 superintendent and 16 constables. The magistrates duly attended a meeting in 1856, 'convened by the Lord Lieutenant and held in the castle of Lincoln in October 1856 for the proper taking into consideration the Act 19 and 20 Vic. Cap. 69 to render more effectual the police in the county boroughs of England and Wales'.

Formal rules were written and all details of recruitment and provision of equipment listed. For example, this was the Lincolnshire profile of a sergeant or constable: 'His age must not exceed 40 years. He must not be less than five feet seven inches high without shoes. He must be a man of general intelligence, able to read and write and keep accounts. He must be certified by a medical practitioner.' He was issued with the following clothing:

One greatcoat with cape and badge

One pair of boots

One pair of shoes

One hat

One stock.

Of course, the ratio of police officers to population varied greatly between counties. In Norfolk, for instance, there were 196 police officers in 1856, giving a ratio to population of 1 per 3,451. In Dorset there were only 12 officers at the time.

By the later Victorian period people were so well informed about the

'Peelers' that letters on the subject were commonly sent to the newspapers, and the opinions voiced in them were often strong, as in this letter to the *Manchester Guardian* in 1873 in response to a discussion on the tendency of constables to arrest anyone supine on the streets:

> We have no wish to be hard upon the constable. Speaking generally, he is not, and cannot be expected to be, a man of discriminating mind, and he usually has a good deal of work on hand – work which, without any fault of character in himself, must tend to develop a cynical faculty. Even a policeman, however, ought to know that men and women may fall powerless to the ground from other causes than excessive drinking.

Studio portrait of Constable Joe Clarke (served 1876–1908). (Reproduced by courtesy of Lincolnshire County Council; from the local studies collection)

This attitude is typical, and well expresses the general development of an ambivalent attitude towards the police, whereby an appreciation of their efforts was tarnished by more negative representations.

In terms of social history within the police structure, looking at constables' orders can be a quick and insightful way to grasp how the ordinary constable fitted in with the larger structures. For instance, the Chief Constable of Cheshire wrote in 1867:

> In all important cases of murder or others of a like serious nature, whenever the solicitor for the prosecution declines to call evidence . . . the Chief Constable requires that immediate reference be made in order to secure authority for such expense . . . such legal advice

will be at once engaged to conduct the examination before magistrates instead of as in some late cases, an incompetent police officer undertaking what is so far beyond his ability, and so inflicting a serious injury on public justice . . .

"She then stood still, and in a clear full voice sang."

The constable's role as carer for the disturbed, from John Ashworth's Strange Tales from Humble Life. *(Author)*

Twentieth-Century Developments

As time went on, the trend was to reduce the number of police forces. A Local Government Act of 1888 replaced the Quarter Sessions as the focus of responsibility for police administration, and also abolished small forces, i.e., those in towns with a population of less than ten thousand. That meant that there were then only 183 forces. Buckingham Constabulary, for instance, was a typical example. It existed from 1836 to 1889 and was very small, with an initial strength of three men and a final one of four. After the 1888 Act it was absorbed into the Buckingham county force.

We can gain some idea of what kind of work provincial policing entailed when we look at some of the notes and memoirs available, such as those of Thomas Smethurst, who served in the Stalybridge Borough Police from 1894 to the 1920s. His annual report for 1912 notes that '33 persons were apprehended for indictable offences, 113 were apprehended and 191 summoned for non-indictable offences'. In that year there were 51 robberies in Stalybridge, 27 inquests and 710 persons summoned for non-payment of rates. Thomas was unusual: the average length of service in his force was eleven and a half years. For the family historian, it is heartening to learn that there are quite a large number of constables' notebooks and memoirs available, but searches for them have to be dogged and determined.

The next large-scale reductions in police forces were effected by the Police Act of 1964 and the Local Government Act of 1972. There had been other rationalisations, too, as in the case of the twenty-six forces on the south coast being amalgamated into just six in 1943. The twentieth century introduced a whole range of specialist personnel into the police, of course, and these have their own records; there was also an expansion of such special forces as those responsible for transport and docks.

Just as new attitudes towards the police developed as time went on, bearing on the reasons why people joined the police, there followed a proliferation of publications (*see* chapter 9) marking a change towards seeing the police as a career; many of the men recruited in the Victorian years did not regard police work as a career. The high rates of resignation suggest that fact. But by the end of the nineteenth century there was a move towards better working conditions and pensions, and with this change came more documentation, meaning that the names of

An early rural police station: Barton on Humber. (Author)

people engaged in police activities both professional and social are easier to find.

Case Study: Richmond Watch and Ward

The Local Studies Collection at Richmond upon Thames Libraries has a wealth of information on the history of watch and ward in the area. They have printed a summary of police development in the town, and Police Sergeant Bernard Brown, formerly of Battersea Police Station, has written a short monograph on the Richmond Division Police. There are also some very old records, going back to the 1780s.

The watch and ward establishments across the country began with the Statute of Westminster of 1285; the idea was that 'ward' referred to day patrols and 'watch' to the night-time patrols. In the earliest period the manorial Court Leet was the judicial area, usually covering three parishes. As early as 1726 there is mention of a lock-up on a map showing a 'Prospect of Richmond'. Regulation began in 1766 and, as with all parishes, the main problem was one of settlement. Every parish had to be vigilant regarding vagrants and travellers within its circumscribed borders. Much of the business at the Quarter Sessions was derived from issues related to vagrancy. The 1766 Act was primarily concerned with poor relief but also covered lighting and watching the streets. It provided for 'The appointment of the Minister, Churchwardens, Justices of the Peace . . . residing in Richmond'.

In 1768 the Richmond Trustees appointed two men to be responsible for watch and ward, and the Vestry, the body controlling these measures, met in a public house until 1790 when a vestry office was built. On 14 April 1786 the Vestry ordered 'that the surveyor give notice to the inhabitants who leave out carriages in the streets and highways . . . that if they cause such obstructions in future the Vestry must be obliged to levy penalties'. A watch-house was erected in 1785 and in 1793 the Vestry worked out a beat system for the watchmen to walk.

Directions to the watchmen were explicit: 'It is ordered by the Vestry that the watchmen do stop all strangers of a suspicious appearance found in the parish, or conveying any articles in carts or otherwise, and not being able to give good account of themselves, and that such suspicious persons be delivered and detained in the custody of the serjeant of the night [sic] . . . to be then taken before a magistrate'. Most watchmen walked the beat or sat with varying degrees of vigilance and are obscured in the fog of history, but in 1821 one night watchman made the headlines when he called on three occupants of a cart to stop; when they ignored him, he fired shots at them and killed one. Luckily, they turned out to be smugglers and so the watchman avoided a murder charge and merely served one year in prison.

The Richmond force was absorbed into the Metropolitan Police in 1840. As well as the watch and ward the borough of Richmond had also had beadles. This was a very ancient office, dating back to the manorial courts, when it was the duty of the beadle to enforce attendance at hearings. He also served writs. In some areas he was simply a constable by another name, but in other places he served as an assistant to the constable.

In terms of finding the names of constables in the watch and ward era, Richmond is an example of a town with some useful records relating to orders and resolutions to a subscription fund. Entries relating to disbursements refer to officers by name, as in these entries for 1785:

1784   £ s d

Sept. 15 Paid Beadle (Mander) for paste and
time going about in sticking up said bills in
this and adjoining parishes   0. 7. 6

Nov. 6. To Thos. Stringer for detecting soldiers
stealing potatoes omitted to be charged before
in this act   1. 1. 0

Chapter 2

CATEGORIES OF RECORD

Superannuation Records and Minute Books

These two categories exemplify the range of materials open to the family historian looking for a police ancestor: minute books are minimal, giving names and short lists of payments made by various councils, vestries and other organisations, whereas superannuation records may often be voluminous. But with minute books there may be surprises, as there tend to be packets of miscellaneous papers attached to minute book records. In Quarter Session minute books, for instance, there may often be accounts of events by chief constables who wrote quarterly reports. There may also be pay sheets. But often the basic record gives a name and a reason for the payments given, such as extra duties or special duties.

In contrast, superannuation records are usually substantial, and they provide the researcher with the opportunity to discover quite detailed information about a constable, including of course his length of service, as well as a career summary, and in the cases of early retirement due to ill health there is often even more information on the person in question. A bare list, as in the following extract from the Hull Police listing officers receiving superannuation on medical grounds, often provides a basis for further work:

Hull Policemen Receiving Superannuation on Medical Grounds, 1851–1866

Policeman	Date pension given	Employment status
Supt. McManus	May 1851	Died in post Apr. 1866
PC Cox	Nov. 1851	Retired on medical grounds

Much more may be gleaned when the medical records and statements or requests for payments are studied. County archives will in most cases have these. Here are some examples from the East Riding Archives based on papers from the East Riding Constabulary superannuation records. First, a general one-off payment:

> Aug. 17 1859
> As required by 19 and 20 Vic. I certify that Police Sergeant William Ford burst a blood vessel in the execution of his duty on the night of 5 June past. I recommend him for a gratuity of 6 months' pay from the superannuation funds.

This is a request giving information about an officer's length of service:

> Superintendent Joseph Young is totally unfit for duty. Vide medical certificate C and D. He has been a PC for 20 and 4/12 years, has served 10 years as a superintendent in this Riding and 14 and 9/12 have been in the present organisation.

Interestingly, this item also offers the sort of extra little details that add depth and character to a name, as the surgeon himself has added an addendum to the medical certificate: 'I may add that he has been under me since 12 July and it was in direct opposition to my wishes that he attended the Assize at York.'

Some accounts give information regarding the areas covered by individuals within a specific constabulary, as in this medical certificate:

> At the general Quarter Session of the peace, 19th day of October, 1873, before the chairman and justices.
> Motion: That there is a recommendation to the Chief Constable that a pension be granted to Superintendent Wilkinson who is incapable from infirmity of body to perform the duties of his office.

R E P O R T

FROM THE

S E L E C T C O M M I T T E E

ON

POLICE SUPERANNUATION FUNDS;

TOGETHER WITH THE

PROCEEDINGS OF THE COMMITTEE,

M I N U T E S O F E V I D E N C E,

A N D A P P E N D I X.

Ordered, by The House of Commons, *to be Printed,*
23 *July* 1875.

The Report from the Select Committee on Police Superannuation Funds, 1875. (Author)

And that a Sergeant or Inspector be appointed to the new lock-up at St John's Wood and also that an additional constable be appointed to the police station at Dairycotes.

By the court,
GEO. LEEMAN
Clerk of the Peace.

Finally, some superannuation requests contain a more exact career summary of an officer, such as this:

Superintendent J.D. Wright has served 37 years. 3 years in Newcastle, 13 as a rural policeman and 21 years as superintendent with the present organisation.

Similarly, George Cordukes's career was:

39 years as a PC – 10 years in the Leeds Borough Police; 6 years as a superintendent with the West Riding Constabulary and 20 years with the present organisation.

It may be seen from this that pension and superannuation payments, from ex gratia to proportional retirement pay, can sometimes provide considerable biographical material.

Personnel and Discipline Books

In the county archives personnel books will be listed as 'Record book of appointments' or 'officer's journal'. Some may be further itemised with such details as abstracts of pay (with dates) for particular areas or divisions. These are merely lists of names, of course, but again they provide a starting-point for more research. There is an immense variety in the usefulness of these records, and they can take various forms, but basically they give lists of staff and offer facts which may lead elsewhere.

But sometimes, as in the case of the Croydon Police records, there are some fine details. Here is an extract from Doris Hobbs' research into 'Service Given to Croydon Police 1829–1840' (*see* Bibliography):

Name	Enrolled	Resigned	Reason	Other Information
Richard Coleman	24.10.29	24.10.38	Persistent drunkenness	Sergeant, formerly Bow Street Patrol
John White	12.9.29	11.4.31	Neglect of duty	None
William Rochford	11.3.35	6.1.36	Not offered place	Formerly Met. on permanent strength
William Wood	4.1.37	11.1.37	Employed one week during Lewis's suspension, labourer.	

Far more informative are discipline books. A typical example is this extract from a discipline book of the Borough of Liverpool Police for 1838, relating to severe criticism expressed by a Commission reporting in line with the 1835 Municipal Reform Act. Between 1 January and 31 December 1838 no fewer than 185 officers were charged with being drunk on duty and 694 with being absent from their beats. Here are some extracts from the Watch Committee records for June 1838:

2/6/1838
Resolved: That John Edwards, No. 65, be fined one shilling for being drunk coming out of a public house when off duty at 12 o'clock on Friday night.

4/6/1838
Ditto: That John Harper, No. 338, be fined one shilling for appearing for duty without his greatcoat.

4/6/1838
Ditto: That William Byrne, No. 217, be fined one shilling for being asleep in a stable at 20 minutes past 2 o'clock on Sunday evening.

Similarly, but with more wide-ranging material, the Police Orders, instituted from the beginning in the Metropolitan Police, contain listings of such things as dismissals, such as these from 1862:

Dismissal.
PC Turner; drunk on duty, losing his truncheon and three keys belonging to premises; and complained of by two civilians for assaulting them with his rattle; pay to 16th.

Reduction.
PC 404, Hammett; making use of an improper remark as the relief was marching for duty; pay as first class to 17th.

Fine.
PC 315 Burnham; admonished for not reporting his having the purse at once. The money returned by the PC proves to be the whole amount lost.

Occurrence Books and Order Books

These were sometimes referred to as incident books or even station diaries. These books were always placed in the stations and were used to record all happenings of any note, from the trivial to the important. Routine duties were also included. For instance, memoirs of constables on routine daily life include such notes as explanations of duties, as in this, written by an anonymous officer serving in the 1850s:

> The ordinary police duty at this time was performed as follows: the night duty was from 10 p.m. to 6 a.m.; the second from 9 a.m. to 3 p.m. at which time the first relief came in again until 10 . . . Frequently in the London season the relief which came off at 9 a.m. had to turn out to attend on her Majesty and Prince Albert when these royal personages arrived or departed from a railway station.

This kind of explanation of the normal work and the special duties covers the spectrum of events recorded in occurrence books. In addition, the occurrence books note the arrival of arrested persons brought to the station, whether they were charged or not, and any officers who were involved; they also give names and ranks, and can help to compile a fuller profile of individual constables. Such books are not difficult to locate as they are, of course, dated, and any lead on a constable from initial meagre information may be further expanded and developed from these books.

Similarly, many stations kept a day book, and there is a perfect example of this from 1845–1846, written by PC Jones of the Denbighshire Constabulary, and researched by Dr F. Clements (*see* Bibliography). Jones included the kind of detail normally found in routine occurrence books, such as,

Report of the Royal Commission on Police Powers and Procedure

Dated 16th March, 1929

Presented by
The Secretary of State for the Home Department
to Parliament by Command of His Majesty

LONDON:
PRINTED AND PUBLISHED BY HIS MAJESTY'S STATIONERY OFFICE.
To be purchased directly from H.M. STATIONERY OFFICE at the following addresses:
Adastral House, Kingsway, London, W.C.2; 120, George Street, Edinburgh;
York Street, Manchester; 1, St. Andrew's Crescent, Cardiff;
15, Donegall Square West, Belfast;
or through any Bookseller.

1929
Price 3s. 0d. Net.

Cmd. 3297

Report of the Royal Commission on Police Powers, 1929. (Author)

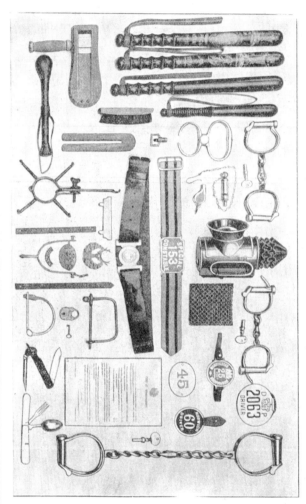
Police equipment as advertised in the Police Journal, *1932. (Author)*

"'ow are yer? Pretty bobbish, eh?"

Public relations – in a riot. Punch cartoon, 1880.

1845
December
I left at 7 a.m. for Burras, 12 p.m.
On duty at residence 6 a.m. and went round the public houses, 12 p.m.

But he includes much fuller details when there was an incident, such as:

> On duty at Burras and Wrexham fair . . . put a man in bridewell
> June 17th. Got the man remanded till the next day. He was
> remanded till the next day. He was discharged, no proof against
> him for stealing a dog . . .

Order books can also provide a wealth of detail about an officer and
are indeed a particularly exciting prospect when they provide details of
a career and also personal qualities. For instance, the record in this
respect for the Lincolnshire Constabulary provides a profile of Sergeant
Dawson. In the section for appointments, promotions and reductions,
we learn that Dawson was appointed in January 1857 as a constable; in
1864 he was promoted to sergeant and in April 1866 he was sergeant
'extra class'. There is a description of him, noting that he was a native of
the village of Welton; he was five feet six and a half inches tall, with
grey eyes, a 'stout' body and 'fresh' complexion. In religion he was
described as a 'churchman' and he was a married man with five children. Dawson had previously been in the army, serving in the 60th
Rifles and the Royal 9th Lincolnshire Militia. Sergeant Dawson was
discharged in December 1873 with a pension of £36 8s per annum, and
he died on 16 May 1884.

Charge Books

Interestingly, calendars of prisoners add a little narrative to the basic
information contained in a charge book. For example, one line in a
calendar reads 'John Clay Oct 13. for stealing one cotton shirt, the property of Matthew Sharman', which gives us the next step from the charge
book, which recorded the constable's name, the alleged offence and the
name of the potential offender. A charge book basically records the
details of the basic facts taken at the station, and sometimes what
happened to the prisoner.

A typical charge book will be a huge and heavy folio volume with

County Borough of Great Grimsby.

CRIMINAL STATISTICS

AND

MISCELLANEOUS RETURNS

FOR THE

YEAR ENDED 31ST DECEMBER, 1911.

GREAT GRIMSBY:

ROBERTS & JACKSON, PRINTERS & STATIONERS, 4 VICTORIA STREET.

1912.

A typical police report from Grimsby, 1911. (Author)

these headings across two pages: Date/name/occupation/charge/
arresting officer/custody record/magistrate/sentence and other notes.
So in these records we have simply the name of the officer involved, as
in this extract from 1861:

> William Wass, shoemaker, arrested by PC 47, Henry Booth, for an
> assault on a constable in the execution of his duty.

Likewise, in 1862 William Wilkinson stole a heifer and was arrested by
Superintendent Horsley. He was given six months in Louth gaol.

The charge books give an enlightening account of the range and nature
of all levels of crime, and they also testify to the high number of assaults
on police. Occasionally an officer was involved in more serious crime, as
in the case of Emma Taylor in 1861 who was charged with feloniously
killing Ann Gray in the parish of Nickenby. She was arrested by a superintendent (not named) but was discharged at the Assizes.

Miscellaneous Sources

The notebooks, journals and records of senior officers present the historian with an extensive catalogue of information, but they are
time-consuming to research. Hunting for an ancestor in these sources
demands great patience and lots of time. The rewards are very high,
though, as these instances will illustrate. In a notebook for 1898, Captain
F.P. Gurney, Chief Constable of the Hull City Police, included descriptions of wanted men, as did H. Osborn, a superintendent working at
Gainsborough in the same year:

> Charlie, alias Feathers, a labourer who stands charged on a
> coroner's warrant with having on the 4th day of June at Long
> Sutton wilfully murdered George Bird . . . He is forty years of age,
> five feet eight high, dark complexion, side whiskers, dressed in a
> light check suit . . . was seen at Barnett on 18th instant. May I ask
> you to make every possible enquiry for this man . . .

More directly useful for the present purpose is a superintendent's
journal. The reason for this is that the superior officers noted and
commented on all kinds of activities involving their staff. In 1891 one
superintendent in Lincolnshire wrote this:

March: attended to office work. Saw PCs Moore and Marshall when in with their weekly reports. PC Warner brought in a tramp for begging as he thought he was wrong in mind. The Rev. Hales remanded him until Monday.

Night – visited conference point at Goodhand's shed at 12 p.m. Conferred with PC Hewson. Thence to conference point at Bird's Yard at 12.30 p.m. Conferred with PCs Rowson and Marshall.

In such journals we also learn about more important matters in a constable's career: 'Received the C.C.'s decision about PC Gilbert. He is dismissed.'

Case Study: County Archive Process and Issues

A visit to the local archives to pursue police ancestors can be a frustrating business. A record that reads something like this will typically be found: Committee Minutes/Chief Constable Records/Establishment Records/Police Routine/Crime Information/Civil Defence. The initial scan of sources may seem promising, but the majority of these are classified as closed, as the century ruling applies: as I write this in March 2008, I can only access police records from before 1908.

Material ranges from photographs to warrant cards and from publicity material to publications such as the *Police Gazette* and officers' journals. Therefore, following the traces of your ancestor's progress and career, once you have located his constabulary and period of service, can mean a determined hunt for all kinds of piecemeal information which has to be collated.

It is possible to apply to the archivist for access to closed documents, but this can be a frustrating experience with a long wait. What this means in effect is that if your subject was in service in the Victorian or Georgian period, covering the first rural forces through to 1908, then you are in luck. After that, the process of enquiry hits some substantial obstacles.

However, persistence is usually rewarded. If you cover the variety of sources listed above, the chances are that in a few hours the person you are looking for will have appeared somewhere, and if they happen to be in the occurrence and order books you may be able to amass quite substantial information.

Practical advice for this hunt for sources can be summarised in this way:

1. Start with the listings on the Police Society/Open University site

2. Write to the archivist or visit the archives to see what is open and what has survived

3. Book a long session so that you can comb through the range at your leisure

4. Try to start with the occurrence books and order books for your period.

Chapter 3

THE NATIONAL ARCHIVES

The website of the National Archives is the best place to start all enquiries into police history and the various archival holdings. In terms of the Metropolitan Police it is particularly rich in resources for the family historian, and every category of record has a user-friendly introductory section explaining the nature of the records. The Royal Irish Constabulary is also well represented here. Navigation around this site is simple and very logically organised, with reference numbers given for each topic as it occurs.

Metropolitan Police Records

Key dates in the historical record of the Metropolitan force are:

- 1829: first establishment
- 1838: the marine police and the Bow Street Runners recommended for amalgamation
- 1842: the detective force established
- 1862: formation of X and W Divisions
- 1872: first police strike.

Before beginning a search, it is helpful to know the nature of the organisation of the force. The original 1829 Act set down the area to be policed by the Peelers as that area within about 7 miles' radius from Charing

NEW POLICE ACT

PASSED IN THE TENTH YEAR OF THE REIGN OF GEORGE IV.

By which the Ancient System of Watch and Ward is abolished, and a general Metropolitan Police established.

New Police Constable.

Illustration from a pamphlet of 1830. (Clifford Elmer)

Cross (with the City of London Police remaining independent). In 1839 this area was extended to cover Middlesex and some parishes in Essex, Surrey, Hertfordshire and Kent. By 1869 the police area was divided into four districts, and each of these had its own divisions. The districts were referred to by number, 1 to 4, and the divisions alphabetically. District 1 included Finsbury, Whitechapel, Stepney, Islington and Thames. All the divisions are listed on the website. The Metropolitan Police was also responsible for the dockyards and other military establishments, and separate records exist for these.

The administration of each division was based around a superintendent, with four inspectors and sixteen sergeants in his team. Certificates of service show that men began their police careers as young as age 18.

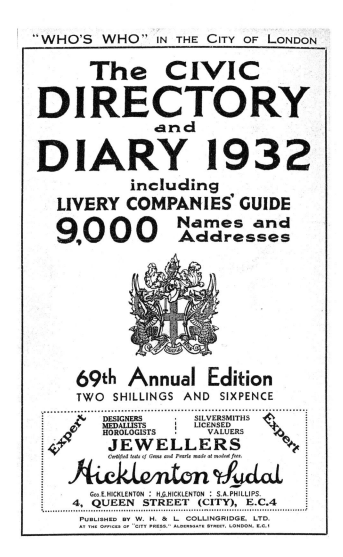

The Civic Directory and Diary *for 1932*. (Author)

Main Records

The staff records at the National Archives are many and varied. The different categories will all give a basis for further work, providing warrant numbers, ranks, divisions and dates of career. These cover numerical registers, alphabetical registers, registers of joiners and attestation ledgers (with signatures of the recruits). Add to these such items as certificates of service, and the narratives of the people concerned begin to deepen. The certificates of service at MEPO 4/361–477 give a fair amount of detail, including movements across the divisions and resignations. The dates of all these vary in scope from the early years through to the mid-twentieth century.

Registers of leavers extend from 1889 to 1947 and give further detail on transfers and resignations, while pension records (as with the county ones covered in the last chapter) can provide details not only from before 1890 (when the payments were discretionary) but also from later periods, and in these will often be found profiles of staff, including their marital status, a physical description and their date and place of birth. Before 1889 you can search the records for a particular name, but after March 1889 you also need to know the approximate date of retirement to use the source effectively.

On the National Archives site and also on the website of the Metropolitan Police (www.met.police.uk/history/index.htm) the specific reference numbers of all these records are given. All you then

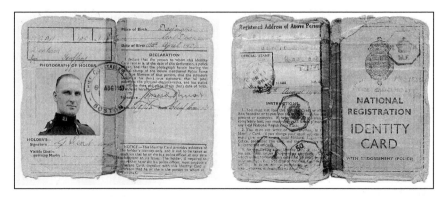

Second World War identity card of PC Geoffrey Denham of Boston Borough Police. (Reproduced by courtesy of Lincolnshire County Council; from the local studies collection)

have to do is go to the relevant sub-heading. For instance, following the reference MEPO 4 for the returns of deaths in the force would lead you to material covering 1829–1889, and for those years this is an open document. The names listed would also be found at MEPO 4/488. In other words, the site is easy to follow when you are trying to locate a person whose dates of service are only approximately known.

Other Sources

There is also a massive database of other sources, including material from the Research Enquiries Room. This source has an index of officers joining the force between 1880 and 1889. There are lists of Special Constables as well (*see* Chapter 7) and these materials are given in MEPO 7 and at MEPO 1/143.

One remarkable resource here is a privately owned index of over 50,000 names of policemen whose names were mentioned in periodicals between 1865 and 1920. The usefulness of this is apparent when one glances at the sheer bulk of material available on the Times Digital Archive, for instance, when a search term of Metropolitan Police with a span of even five years is used. The range of stories is immense, and this can add a fuller narrative to a biography, of course. Some references are found by sheer serendipity, for example if a constable happens to be involved in an important case or something related to sport and leisure.

Although police orders are closed for fifty years (sources covering 1829–1989), obviously the earlier ones are accessible, and these give details of officers pensioned, promoted and dismissed, as explained in the previous chapter. An index compiled from these police orders has been compiled and is available at MEPO 7/42/51.

Finally, there are divisional records and correspondence series, but once again there is a closure of at least seventy-five years on these. But there are records of honours and awards and these may be viewed. In MEPO 2/1300 there is a list of awards for 1909–1912.

Royal Irish Constabulary

This was an armed police force, formed in 1836, and the first recruits were found from among the tenant farmers. The RIC was very unpopular in the nineteenth century as it was used to enforce land evictions, and was an intelligence source for the British establishment at Dublin Castle. Before 1914 recruitment had notably declined, and then in 1919 an official negotiating body was formed with the National Union of Police and Prison Officers. The RIC ceased to exist in 1922. Service records of RIC men up to 1922 are at the National Archives, but these are not public records. For family history purposes, the most positive approach is to try local records.

The most useful starting-point is to consult J. Herlihy's *The Royal Irish Constabulary: A Complete Alphabetical List of Officers and Men 1816–1922*,

The entrance to Dublin Castle.
(Author)

which has some summaries of service details. Document references at HO 184 may add to these, where possible (using Home Office rather than MEPO references). Chapter 11 gives more on this topic.

Metropolitan Police Historical Museum

There is some difficulty involved in using the records at this museum, and in fact the incomplete records for various divisions have recently been moved to the London Metropolitan Museum by way of the City of London Corporation Archives. In other words, the situation has been something of a mess in terms of a system being available that would be helpful to the family historian. But the Access to Archives scheme has meant that gradually the records are being rationalised. It is still possible (as of February 2008, according to the National Archives' website) to contact both the museum at New Scotland Yard and the Wapping Police Station Museum, but it seems as though this is being phased out.

The best plan when tracing Metropolitan Police staff, then, is to start with the Access to Archives database and then go to service lists. From that point, the first step is to search for a name and warrant number. The London Metropolitan Police History site has a listing of the series of warrant numbers for the years between 1829 and 2000. The table on that site gives the series of numbers for each year, so that 1839, for example, extends from 13460 to 15760. If the researcher knows the warrant number of a particular officer, this chart will give the year in which that person joined the force. Warrant numbers between 154639 and 154774 were for transfers from Essex Police in 1966. Women police had a separate series of warrant numbers between 1919 and 1993, ending at number 9994.

There are also more specific lists of researchers and sites that might be approached for additional details on a subject. For instance, the roll of honour website is a good source: www.policememorial.org.uk. There is also the Spike Hughes database. Spike, who died in 2006, compiled a list of officers serving from the last years of the nineteenth century up to 1915. The names entered were sourced from police orders, so the site is thorough and gives useful information. Also useful is the organisation Friends of the Metropolitan Police Historical Collection, located at www.friendsofMetHistory.co.uk.

Chapter 4

ALMANACS AND REFERENCE

Th-here are several general reference works which provide a mine of information in list form. The most comprehensive, such as *Whitaker's Almanac*, list chief constables in London, while the standard reference work is *The Police and Constabulary Almanac*. The latter is still printed annually, and has been produced in an unbroken series since 1858.

What You Will Find in the Almanac

The police almanac was first printed in Manchester by Thomas Sowler at St Ann's Square. In the early years its industrious compiler was Edwin Shepherd of Blackburn. In the early and classic form, the almanac printed information on county and borough forces, with senior officers, stations and divisions. It therefore provides a profile of senior management as well as the geography and structure of each force. Magistrates, lords lieutenant and sheriffs for counties are also there, so the publication gives the substance of the whole criminal justice system at the time. Contents up to 1920 in relation to police work and criminal administration include: governors and chaplains of gaols; railway police forces and senior officers; Police Mutual Assurance; the police orphan home location and officers; chairmen of police committees; chairmen of Quarter Sessions; coroners; and general police statistics.

For the family historian, the 1899 edition for example has all this infor-

The Police and Constabulary Almanac. (Reproduced by permission of R. Hazell & Co.)

POLICE AND CONSTABULARY ALMANAC

including Fire Brigades & Ambulance Services
Civil Defence and Courts of Law

OFFICIAL REGISTER

2008

being the fifty-seventh year of
the reign of Her Majesty
Queen Elizabeth the Second

This Almanac is obtainable direct
from the publisher only

R HAZELL & Co

mation with the addition of such details as 'legalised police cells'. A typical entry is this, from Leeds 19:

Chief Constable: F.T. Webb (late 12th Royal Lancers)

Town Hall

Police surgeons, Drs G.H. Heald and E. Ward.

A Division: Chief Superintendent Arthur Dalton at Millgarth

B Division: Amos Mason at Hunslet

C Division: Samuel Lincoln at Sheepscar

D Division: Frank Forster at Kirkstall Road

E Division (fire brigade) Henry R. Barker, Park Street.

In the main alphabetical listings of chief constables, these are typical entries from 1899:

BUCKS. Major Otway Mayne, Aylesbury

HALIFAX, York. W.R. Charles Pole.

From 1858 details of Irish policing were included in the almanac. The information increased towards the end of the Victorian period, sometimes even giving the names of sergeants; after 1920 the scope widened to include a gazetteer of police stations. Another source available in these publications – material that enriches the whole area of study – is the advertisements. Here we learn about police armourers, for instance, and clothes outfitters. Especially interesting are the ancillary notes, such as the advertisement placed by Nathaniel Druscovich in 1882 for the British and Foreign Enquiry Office (a private detective agency). This was a former Scotland Yard man who had fallen from grace after the scandal known as 'The Trial of the Detectives' in 1877.

In 1906 the Manchester Courier Ltd took over production of the almanac, and then in 1919 the current publishers, R. Hazell, took it over.

Access to copies before 1908 is straightforward at record offices but later copies may be difficult. There is a complete run of all editions at the Police Staff College at Bramshill House, Hartley Wintney, Hampshire (established in 1948), but they may not be borrowed and visits to read them have to be arranged.

Other Reference Works

As with all matters pertaining to special reference, the diversity is part of the problem, and many of the sources are hard to find. But making a first search in such publications as parochial documents can turn up unexpected material, as in the documents for the East Riding of Yorkshire, which contain constables' accounts for 1805–1828 and a constable's book covering 1809–1843. But in terms of major works, one useful source is a civic directory.

A civic directory includes major figures, offices and responsibilities, including staff within the criminal justice system. The police staff are classed along with such people as court officials and city officers. There is sometimes a very full staff listing. For instance, the London *Civic Directory and Diary* for 1932 has this summary of City of London Police staff in that year:

Chief Office: Old Jewry

Commissioner – Lieut-Col. Sir Hugh Turnbull KBE JP

Assistant Commissioner – John Stark CBE

Chief Superintendent, Detective Department – E. Thompson

Chief Inspector, Detective Department – E. Nicholls

Chief Inspector, Executive Department – E. Dallimore

Chief Inspector, Clerical Department – G.H. Doo

In addition, we are told that the permanent staff at headquarters included: Sgt C. Austen, Sgt A.J. Nunn, Sgt J. Martin and Sgt E. Budden (the latter of the City Reserve).

Of a different nature are the materials in official reports and enquiries. For instance, in parliamentary reports it is possible to find assorted papers based on interviews with staff. In 1836 the first report by the future Metropolitan Commissioner was issued, and from that date other enquiries have taken place, each offering a mixed assortment of sources. The papers from the very first report are at the National Archives under reference numbers HO 73.2 to HO 73.9 and there is correspondence at HO 72.3 to 73.7.

Hue and Cry and *Police Gazette*

These two titles are classic police publications, produced for the profession and giving details of crimes, locations, victims and the process of law involved. Their origins lie in the eighteenth century, with the work of Henry Fielding, the novelist and justice of the peace. He started *The Covent Garden Journal* in 1752 and so set the precedent for a police publication that would assist in streamlining communication across the city. The substance of this type of periodical was set out in this advertisement from 1754:

Whereas many thieves and robbers daily escape justice for want of immediate pursuit, it is therefore recommended to all persons, who shall henceforth be robbed on the highway or in the streets, or whose shops or houses shall be broken open, that they give immediate notice thereof, together with as accurate description of the offenders as possible, to John Fielding esq. at his house in Bow Street . . .

John Fielding was Henry's brother. Despite his blindness, he was very effective as a magistrate. Later in their careers, the Fieldings also produced two other publications, the *Quarterly Pursuit* and the *Weekly Pursuit*. Then in 1786 Sir Samson Wright produced *Hue and Cry* which had become by 1795 *The Hue and Cry and Police Gazette*.

In 1828 the publication became simply *The Police Gazette* but there was an overlap. An issue for November 1829 still has *Hue and Cry* in the title. But by that date it had become a folded imperial sheet, with regular listings of army deserters as well as entries on specific crimes. This is a typical entry from early Victorian times:

Stolen, on Monday night, the 9th instant, from the person of a Gentleman, in the pit of Covent Garden Theatre, one gold watch, with gold dial and burnished figures, also a gold seal and key.

Much additional material contained in these publications enlarges on what might be found in a police charge book, such as this example from Marlborough Street office: 'GEORGE KEMP, re-examined on suspicion of stealing thirty pictures, of the value of four hundred pounds, the property of John Hewison. Remanded until Thursday next.'

For the family historian, the *Gazette* offers a massive resource but of course it is not indexed. As L.A. Waters commented in a Police History Society booklet: 'With each item there is also given the name and place of office of a senior officer as a contact. This valuable and largely untapped source contains millions of names but is not indexed.' The British Library has copies of the *Gazette* from a range of dates in the nineteenth century, but thanks to some useful research by Les Waters in 1986, we have a summary of places where copies are available throughout the country. His listings are in *The Journal of the Police History Society*, no. 1 (1986), 30–41.

Chapter 5

THE CITY OF LONDON POLICE

Survey of Files and Materials

The history of the City of London Police, which was independent of the Metropolitan force from the very beginning of professional policing, embraces a vast array of cases, ranging from financial misdoings to river crime, and even an involvement in the Jack the Ripper murders in Whitechapel and the siege of Sidney Street of 1911. Some of the first City detectives were known to Charles Dickens and he wrote about them in his periodicals. The force has particular records and materials of great interest to the family historian, notably a rich history of sporting, recreational and charity work, all with artefacts, manuscripts and photographic sources.

The main archives are held at the Corporation of London Record Office, but there are also materials at the Wood Street museum, although application has to be made to the curator here. The Corporation of London controls the usual local authority functions of such a body, running its own police force and administering the Central Criminal Court. At the Corporation Office there are orders and regulations, chronological series of orders and reports, incidents manuals, publications, honours lists, photographs and lists of special constables. But most importantly, this is the location of the lists of officers and warrant numbers since 9 April 1832, with personal files for some 95 per cent of the officers of the City force.

There is a certain degree of chaos in the force records here. There has

The famous blue lamp, outside Wood Street station, City of London Police. (Author)

been a transfer of the staff records from the National Archives, and on the Access to Archives listings of holdings at the Corporation there is at the moment (March 2008) no coherent listing of these, although there is a massive body of material relating to such secondary topics as honours lists and particular items such as a City of London Freedom Certificate for William Summerbell, a sergeant in the City Police.

Although there are other organisations and websites whose work overlaps on this material and whose information may be useful, the Corporation at the Guildhall must be the starting-point for City Police research. Sites on the internet with relevant interests are listed in the Bibliography.

Experience has taught me that the City force is one of those organisations which offers a rich and diverse range of sources and materials to the historian generally, but for family research you will need time and persistence despite the bulk of relevant material being to hand in one place. But the occurrences and orders are there, ready for the usual enquiry, found at ref. CLA/048/AD/11. There are also, because of the nature and position of the City force, several areas of importance in national history that impinge on the stories of the City personnel: such matters include the General Strike of 1926, the anarchist troubles of the Edwardian period and indeed the first police strike of 1918–1919.

The Scope of the Records

For the above reasons, the scope of the CLA records is immense, if somewhat chaotic. If your ancestor was notable for, say, his sporting prowess, or for his involvement in any public honours or good works for the charity schools, your research will bring you a fairly substantial biographical narrative; otherwise there will be a bare record of dates with promotions and so on. A typical example of the range of sources is the ambulance service, an important part of the force since its most celebrated commissioner, Nott-Bower, came to the city from Liverpool at the turn of the nineteenth century, bringing with him the concept of the police ambulance service; the papers of that service are at CLA/048/AD/11/024. They cover the years 1907–1949 and have correspondence from the period 1944–1949 as well.

A great deal of attention has been given to collecting and preserving these records, largely through the dedication of individuals such as Roger Appleby, recently retired from his duties as curator at Wood Street. Perhaps not unfairly, more attention has been given to preserving records of ceremony and ritual than to other more everyday events, but the benefit of this is that if your ancestor was awarded a medal for bravery then the material will be substantial and there will almost certainly be photographs. Mr Appleby also collected a series of leaflets on notable events such as the awarding of sports and gallantry medals and these are still at Wood Street.

There is also some material at the London Metropolitan Archives, but this is largely restricted to court records, so for example, detective officers and constables involved in cases from Surrey or Middlesex would figure here, as in the detective story ending this chapter. The London Metropolitan Archives offers a family history search service and their holdings may be checked at their 'London Generations' database. If you decide to use this search service, then the charge is currently £35 per hour. For this, the service provides a listing of all sources used and a transcript or copy of relevant information. The service returns information after approximately a month's wait. This archive also provides a guide to family history at this centre, and the user may download a form entitled 'The Guide to Family History at the LMA'.

The best way forward, then, in locating ancestors from the City force, is to start with the main lists and warrant numbers at the Corporation records, and then to follow through with the dates acquired to enlarge on information from any other sources. For instance, if an officer was active in a certain period, then the chances are that some aspects of the larger context will have impinged on his career. At this point it is worth stressing the importance of newspaper data as well. Because the City area covered only a square mile and the force was of limited size, there is a reasonably high chance that within the Times Digital Archive there will be some references to a large number of officers, from constables upwards. For instance, the Cannon Street murder of 1866 provides a voluminous range of descriptions from the newspapers about that event, and entries such as these are numerous:

> Henry Hunt, a policeman in M Division, deposed that on the 4th February last the deceased showed him the letter . . . (27 April)
> I opened the street door to look for a policeman, and City policeman 467 came to my assistance . . . (19 April)
> On their return, Mr Superintendent Forster, who was present to watch the case on behalf of the City authorities . . . (14 April)

In addition, as initial hearings for all crimes committed in the City were heard at the Guildhall, there are detailed and extensive accounts of investigations there, and within these reports the reader can learn a great deal about the social and professional history of the City Police, with names given in most cases. For instance, in 1865 there was a spate of robberies from jewellers and one, involving Walkers of Hercules Passage, led *The Times* to report on the workings of the beat system and how constables worked in the immediate area, as in this extract from a report: 'Inspector Hamilton, chief of the City detective police, deposed that on the Monday morning he and other police officers made minute examination of the premises of Mr Walker. He found an entrance had been made into the shop by a hole cut in the floor . . .'

There were just 796 men in the City force in 1877. Expanding on the social history around their daily lives could include, for instance, the City Police Convalescent Home (which also catered for soldiers in the Boer War); this is one further source of information, as is the City of London Police Mission. Clearly, *The Times* and other newspapers were keen to report positive images of police activity, and these institutions, along with the various social and cultural activities, present the family historian with a wealth of information, and there is a high chance that a relative may figure in reports. Such items as this obituary from *The Times* on 13 February 1936 is entirely typical:

> Mr Charles Berg, of Harold Road, Leytonstone, who was shot in the throat when he grappled with a man who attempted to murder Mr Leopold Rothschild in the City in 1912, has died . . . He was already a pensioned police officer and at the time was a keeper at the main entrance to the bank . . .

As a coda to information sources for the City Police, mention must be made of Rob Jerrard's website, www.rjerrard.co.uk/law/city, because Mr Jerrard is a historian of the force, but also has a network of various relatives who have memorabilia and who write about the City Police. One of the most useful of these for present purposes is a book by Dora Tack, *My Brixton Childhood: Memories of a City of London Policeman's Daughter*. Dora Tack is the daughter of Percy Warwick Ellis. Other memoirs of the City Police that are worth finding are listed in the Bibliography.

Case Study: A Detective Story

If your police ancestor was in the detective department, then the sources mentioned earlier in this chapter, the court records at the London Metropolitan Archives, could present you with some fascinating information. One well-documented example concerns the murder of a detective. The man in question was Charles Thain, a man who had been fatally shot by a prisoner on board the *Caledonia* while the ship was in dock in 1857. The account of the trial is in the sessions of the Surrey Cases for 1857–1858 and involves two detectives (Thain and Jarvis) and two City constables, Edwin Hill (policeman no. 415) and Thomas Cunnocks (no. 451).

The drama culminates in Thain giving evidence from his death-bed, with a statement that,

> On the 19th Nov. instant I had the prisoner in custody in Hamburg, and this day week we sailed in the *Caledonia* for London. We were in the cabin by ourselves – which I had the key of – he complained of being ill . . . About twenty minutes before 4 o'clock I got up and left the cabin. I returned and he was sitting on a folded carpet stool . . . I had a mackintosh cape in my hand and while I was in the act of folding it away, he stood up and fired at me – I felt wounded on the right nipple and cried out 'Murder!'

The killer, Christian Sattler, was found guilty and hanged.

Chapter 6

THE SPECIAL CONSTABULARY

A Short History

Special constables, often jocularly called 'hobby bobbies', have been a part of the police structure since the reign of Charles II. In 1673 an act was passed which made it possible for any man to be called on to fulfil the role of 'temporary police officer'. In the following years lists of 'specials' were kept, and they were ready to be called principally for use in exceptional circumstances such as in radical protest, street violence and even the threat of open revolution. In the Georgian period they appear frequently in the social history, most notably in deplorable episodes such as the Peterloo Massacre in Manchester in 1819, when soldiers confronted and attacked civilians at a public meeting.

The most formative legislation in this context came in 1831 with the Special Constables Act, by which these constables were given full powers and equipment to put them on an equal footing with regular officers. Then in 1834 (and largely in a climate of fear created by the Chartist movement) the specials were allowed to move outside their own parishes to be effective. For instance, a report in *The Times* of a Chartist disturbance in Bradford in May 1848 notes that 'The police and specials then succeeded in capturing 18 of the most active of the Chartists'. The figure of the voluntary Special Constable also emerged from this legislation. Obviously, whenever there was trouble of a political nature, or crime waves too extensive to handle with the normal manpower, the specials were sworn in; during the 1830s 'Swing Riots' across the eastern counties, for example, the Chief Constable of Essex employed a number of temporary officers.

In the first half of the twentieth century specials were very important. At the end of the First World War, a medal was established for service as a special, and indeed the specials had played an important part in various defence actions during the war, including taking part at one time in the capture of a Zeppelin. This shows how prominent the use of specials was by this time; they had gradually become more widespread

Rhys, M.P.. and Messrs. Flood and Bevir, of the Colonial Office, have arrived back from an extensive tour of British Possessions in West Africa.

REGENT'S PARK CLOSED

Regent's Park is now closed, and is being used for public purposes.

A NORMAL BUS SERVICE

A conspicuous example of how a public service is being carried on even in the present circumstances is furnished by the East Surrey Traction Company, Limited, whose headquarters is at Reigate. Since the strike began the Company's offices have been besieged by volunteers for duty either as drivers or conductors, and as a result the whole of the 140 East Surrey buses are now on the road. All routes were in operation even yesterday.

CIVIL CONSTABULARY

PAID WHOLE-TIME "SPECIALS"

The Deputy Civil Commissioner announces his decision to organise a further force of citizens to help the Metropolitan and City Police. This new force will be designated "The Civil Constabulary Reserve," and will be a paid whole-time force of sworn-in special constables organised in units, wearing plain clothes, but supplied with armlets, steel helmets, and truncheons.

The following will be eligible to join : Officers and other ranks of the Territorial Army and the senior contingent of the Officers' Training Corps, and ex-military men who can be vouched for at Territorial Army Units Headquarters. Age limit 50 years. Daily pay as follows : Commander 10/-. Inspector 7/6, Sergeant 6/-, Constable 5/-. Recruiting offices in all drill halls of the City of London and County of London Associations.

SATURDAY'S CRICKET

SURREY v AUSTRALIANS—Australians 301 for 6 (Taylor 76, Woodfull 87 not out).
MIDDLESEX v ESSEX—Essex 246 (Freeman 62, Russell 122 not out). Middlesex 5 for no wicket.
WORCESTER v SOMERSET—Worcester 225 : Somerset 14 for 2.
GLOUCESTER v LANCASHIRE—Lancashire 145, Gloucester 79 for 1.
DERBYSHIRE v YORKSHIRE—Yorkshire 170, Derby 76 for 2.
WARWICKSHIRE v HAMPSHIRE—Warwick 266, Hampshire 16 for 2.
LEICESTERSHIRE v GLAMORGAN—Leicestershire 195, Glamorgan 37 for 1.
NOTTINGHAMSHIRE v SUSSEX—Nottingham 232, Sussex 62 for 4.

A constabulary announcement during the 1926 General Strike. (Daily Worker)

after the 1856 Act establishing borough forces and thus completing professionalisation. Historian Clare Leon explained the basis of this change in the *Journal of the Police History Society*, no. 5 (1990):

> . . . even though the majority of areas had introduced paid police forces by the late 1850s special constables were still being widely deployed . . . The principle of annually appointing special constables in the boroughs was restated by the 1882 Municipal Corporations Act. In addition, various occupational groups were still being sworn in, in order to give them additional police powers.

This makes sense in the context of such events as the dock strikes and the growth of trade union militancy. Even earlier, in the years between 1843 and 1854, as research by Peter Bramham on Keighley in West Yorkshire has shown, there was a large body of men available and from all kinds of occupations. Bramham found that of the 221 men sworn in as specials, 70 were farmers, 43 shopkeepers and 27 textile manufacturers, but there were also clerks, tailors and three gentlemen among the recruits (*see* Bibliography).

By 1923 permanent special constabularies were introduced. But essentially, the use of specials has always been supplementary, and there was never any intention to replace permanent staff.

Records

Again, the first step outside London is a visit to the relevant County Record Office. The special constables will be included in the general lists under 'Constabulary'. For instance, as Fred Feather noted in an article on special constables, in his local record office there are 'at least seven different organisations which would have included specials in their line-up' (*Family and Local History Handbook,*

Sergeant Joseph Fitch served with the Special Constabulary of Fleet from 1948 to 1972. (Reproduced by courtesy of Lincolnshire County Council; from the local studies collection)

9.) Here, Mr Feather was of course referring to the smaller constabularies before rationalisation.

At the regional and local level, the sources available are varied. Sometimes the material is substantial and presents a detailed view across the spectrum of the lives and duties of specials, as in the archives from the Sussex Police Authority held at Lewes. Here, at catalogue reference SPA, the following material is listed:

Standing orders and instructions

Unregistered files of a chief constable

Correspondence and reports, including notes on the special constabulary

Photographs of a special constable, c. 1930

Civil Defence and administration for Bexhill

Personal papers of a constable from Brighton Special Constabulary

In addition, there is also a file on Alfred Archibald Fordham, a special constable serving with Uckfield Division.

What may be observed from this is the element of serendipity involved: some material gives biographical information that would delight a family history researcher, while other sources are wholly administrative. At the West Yorkshire Archives, for example, for Sowerby Bridge Special Constabulary, there is a minute book and correspondence, so there would be plenty of named officers there, and similarly at Devon Record Office there are various personal papers, including the diary of Sergeant S. Wide, along with a book recording the special duties relating to the Hemlock Group, Devon Special Constabulary. The good news is that there is a vast store of material across the country on special constables.

At the National Archives the specials used to complement the Metropolitan Police are published in Police Orders at MEPO 7. Also, a nominal roll for 1875 provides a list of officers sworn in to supplement the regular force, and this is at MEPO 2/143. This gives the date of appointment, place of work and the name of a recognised official sponsor for the candidature.

For the City of London Police the Corporation of London has some intriguing items, at CLA/048/ADE/11. These include a register of citizens of suitable age and physical fitness for duties in the event of an emergency. These registered members were formed into divisions and arrangements were made for calling them and swearing them in if needed. There were 2,014 specials in 1939 on the outbreak of the Second World War. In 1947 a history of the force was produced, with Commandant William Penman at the centre of the story. Also included is the journal called *The Rattle* (from the 1950s).

All this reflects the use of special constables during the war – both men and women – and some earned the Defence Medal. After the war some officers naturally converted to full-time staff, not least because of the shortages of manpower caused by the war.

Finally, there is something to be said for a researcher writing to the Special Commandant at the local constabulary in order to find out about any amateur chronicler of the local special constabulary. This may well elicit some information and possibly a very useful contact with files and records already compiled. This brings us to the subject of unofficial records. One useful source here is the memorials created in many areas

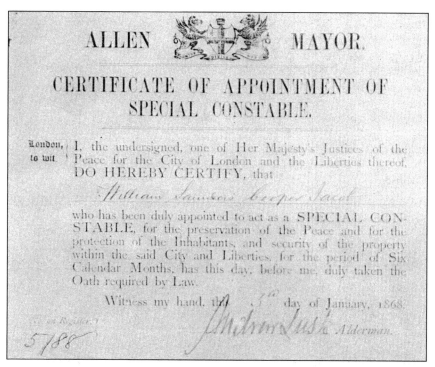

Certificate of appointment for a special constable. (City of London Police Archives)

The police out with the army during a dock strike in 1911. (Laura Carter)

of the country to specials after the First World War. In Essex, for example, a few dozen of these scrolls, once placed in magistrates' courts, have survived and are in the police museum at Chelmsford, as Fred Feather relates in the article referred to above.

Case Study: The Police Strike (1919) and War Service

Very often national news can generate names and events relating to family history research, and a good case in point is the Police Strike in London at the end of the First World War. During the years of that war large numbers of special were recruited. In the T Division Special Constabulary for 1915, for instance, covering the H/N Sub-division of Twickenham, Teddington, Hampton and Sunbury, there were 435 specials, including all ranks from inspectors to constables, although it has to be noted that there were 137 resignations that year also. As noted by G.W. Kettlewell, Chief Inspector of H/N Sub-Division, the 'first attestations of Special Constables' took place on 17 August 1915, 'held for the purpose of adding to the strength and to supply deficiencies caused by the enlistment, physical disability or other resignations of Special Constables . . .'.

These staff were certainly needed when the strike began. The worst affected areas were London and Liverpool in 1918–1919. In London widespread unrest developed and a strike was called by an unofficial union (strike action by the police was one of the central issues); the first strike was called in 1918 and was well supported; for the second strike, the following year, the turnout was low and the unofficial strikers found themselves in trouble. The Police Act of 1919 established the Police Federation and the National Union of Police and Prison Officers (NUPPO) was doomed to failure. But there had been considerable disruption, and against that background the participation of the specials was remarkable.

On 18 June 1919 a permanent reserve was established for the Metropolitan Police, so even though the war was over there was still a definite need for the special constabulary. A circular sent to all Chief Constables in 1918 had recommended that the adoption of specials and the specials' workloads were to be stepped down after the war. Nevertheless, when the strike came along, they were in demand.

But there was also war service in general. The special constabulary had played a very important role, and on 13 June 1919 some 17,400 specials were demobilised from service, although of course many were retained. The point is that it was a very public acknowledgement of their role and illustrates how highly they were valued. It was an occasion for strict protocol: 'Only officers and men on the active service roll may take part . . . For the information of those taking part, it is notified that all ranks will parade in inspection parade order, without truncheons, and officers will not carry sticks.' *The Times* noted that, 'Many of [them] will probably join the Metropolitan Special Constabulary Reserve . . .'.

Given their high public profile, it will come as no surprise to learn that the newspapers at the time printed the names of all constables who received special mentions for their war service. These names, with their respective divisions, were all printed in *The Times* of 14 February 1919. They had been 'brought to the notice of the Home Secretary for valuable services rendered'. For instance, we learn that the men from G Division so honoured were: 'Ass. Comm. W.H. Erskine, Ch. Insp. H.A. Lowe, Sub-Insp. L.D. Krall, Sgt R. Clarke and Sgt C.T.W. Rafa'.

Chapter 7

THE PALESTINE POLICE FORCE

A Short History

After the Sykes–Picot Agreement of 1917, which established Britain's importance in the settlement of the Middle East balance of power and gave her an on-going policing role in Egypt, confirmation was made in the 1920 Mandate for Palestine to fall within the British remit. The Palestine Police Force was therefore created, officially existing from 1 July 1920. It was to last for twenty-eight years.

The Palestine Police had the very difficult job of keeping law and order and preventing looting. They took over the role from the Turks, as the Turkish Empire had been allied with the Germans in the First World War. As a recent writer, H.J. Godsave, has written in *The Police History Society Journal*:

> The Turkish system remained in force in the early days, especially in gathering information and confessions, but the police under the British system had to be seen to be servants of the public. . . . The Palestine Police had its own particular problem in keeping law and order with the multi-racial, multi-religious population and the numerous holy sites . . .

There is no shortage of memoirs in print from former policemen in that force, and the sources for family historians are many and varied, though somewhat dispersed. But another dimension of interest here is that many of these personnel returned home after 1948 and went into police work in Britain. In January 1948 the *Evening News* reported that Deputy Superintendent J.A.S. Adolf was already in Britain, trying to find work for returning officers from Palestine: 'Adolf anticipates that many of the men will join other police forces in this country and in the Empire'. Adolf's grandson, writing recently in *Practical Family History* magazine, wrote, 'By February, the *Evening Standard* reported that my grandfather had already found 1,000 jobs for Palestine Policemen in police forces'. J.A.S. Adolf eventually found work for almost all the former Palestine policemen, and himself took a job as head of security at Falmouth docks.

The Middle East Centre

Initially the service records of the Palestine Police were put together by the Colonial Office, and then they were held at the Overseas Development Administration. What happened after that was rather chaotic, because it was decided that they were not eligible to be acquired by the National Archives and so they were split, some going to Bristol and some to Oxford. At Oxford, in St Anthony's College, the Middle East Centre holds service record cards, given under the Public Records (Presentation of Records) Instrument no. 8.

These record cards are only useful if the person's service number is known, as they are not organised alphabetically by surname. Some have photographs. Each card has a large number of headings for information, and so in many cases there is a great deal of data to be acquired about the person's work in Palestine. Apart from basic details such as place of birth, nationality and date of enlistment, there are invaluable sections for other aspects, such as: education; appointment, promotions and reductions; divisions served in (with transfer dates); qualifications (most studied Arabic); signature; medical history; family register; commendations; and punishments.

The MECA produces plenty of guidance material, and there is a summary of sources on the internet. This notes also the related archives such as the Brebber Collection (military court documentation) and the Kermack Collection, a resource containing a memoir of work done by the Palestine Judicial Service.

In the main collection the material is substantial, and the website guide lists the main items alphabetically, so a typical entry is: 'CANNINGS, Victor Henry Douglas (b. 1919) GB165–0386.' Papers relating to his service in the British mandate Palestine Police include a police identity card, the Criminal Code Ordinance for 1936, several Palestine Police magazines from 1939 to 1947, three photographs of the Palestine Police cricket team and a Certificate of Discharge from the police. Very interestingly, there is also an oral history interview that was carried out in 2006 covering Canning's service in the Palestine Police. Also included is a booklet on Jerusalem promoting the work of the Jewish Agency and press cuttings covering bombings and the deteriorating security situation in Palestine in the period 1944–1946, and an essay on Cannings' later cricket career, dated 1958.

The MECA oral history project has added another fascinating dimension to our knowledge of the Palestine Police Force, and in the list of items there are several summaries of these interviews, which were based on formal questionnaires. A typical example, by John Card, lasts for over an hour and covers his three years of service in considerable detail.

Special Note:
Access to service record cards is of course subject to the Data Protection legislation. Access can only be granted in line with this legislation, therefore applications to the archivist in this context are essential.

British Empire and Commonwealth Museum

This is in Bristol, at Temple Meads. The museum has around 8,000 service files arranged by surname, and they replicate the information found in Oxford. But in addition there is other material, such as progress reports, training school reports and salary details. Another useful document that may be available is an attestation paper – a questionnaire filled in when the person joined, and this should include a photograph. Also available is pension information, which is always a useful source. These are found at reference number 2004/039/- in the catalogue.

Interestingly, there are other documents under internet address: www.bris.ac.uk/Depts/History/Staff/duffy.htm and here there are some papers relating to particular individuals in the force.

National Archives and Other Sources

The National Archives, although not holding any service records, does have material that may be valuable for the family history researcher. As usual, the online catalogue offers a summary and guide to these, under the heading 'Colonial Office papers'. This is a treasure-trove of the social history of the force, even covering applications for the use of camels, then located at the famous Bertram Mills' Circus (1934). The main holdings here are:

Foreign Office papers (for instance, on recruitment)

Passenger lists provided by the Board of Trade (these contain lists of officers and their families)

Mr F.C. Brookes of the Kenya Police. (Author's collection)

War Office papers

Details from British organisations on employment of ex-Palestine Police officers

Pensions information from Treasury records

Correspondence

A very rich source of information is the Palestine Police Old Comrades Association, based in Nottingham (*see* resources list with Bibliography). The PPOCA has produced various newsletters, always a fine source of biographical details, and they hold personal papers of officers from the 1920s to the 1990s. The official historian of the organisation is Edward Horne and his material is also held by the PPOCA. Some of the special features of the Old Comrades website are a gallery of commandants and police inspector generals, and also an account of the duties performed in each district.

In these archives there are quantities of uncatalogued items, and according to Anthony Adolf this source extends to some fifty boxes.

Case Study: Police in the Empire

One of the less common enquiries in the history of the police is the family history of officers serving in India and other outposts of empire. There are numerous books on the police organisation in India, for instance, clearly the major destination for British police who were drafted in to help organise and discipline the native forces. A typical chronicle of such men, *The Bombay City Police* by S.M. Edwardes, who was Commissioner of Police in that city, gives an account of the important figures in that story, stretching from 1672 to 1916. His book was published in 1923 and includes accounts of several major administrators such as Sir Frank Souter, H.G. Gell and Lieutenant-Colonel W.H. Wilson.

G.G.B. Iver of the Indian Police wrote a similar account in 1919, *In An Indian District*, which gives a clear summary of how the colonial police operated throughout the Indian subcontinent, covering the rise of the magistracy, police administration and life within the government organisation. Any researcher with ancestors who went out to serve there would find this an excellent introduction to the force in which the ancestor served. The force stemmed from legislation passed in 1861, which created twenty-three districts. Of course, in these cases the ancestor will be either a senior officer or an administrator, and in some

*Lieutenant-Colonel
W.H. Wilson of the
Bombay Police.
(Author's
collection)*

cases an ex-army man with duties in recruitment and discipline. Mr Iver's little book is full of advice for British officers going out to work in the force, such as:

With your language well in hand, try to get acquainted on friendly terms with leading men, official or otherwise. You will find that they respond more than readily to courtesy and friendliness. The Indian values these beyond words, and you will have gained the first step in securing his assistance and co-operation in criminal work.

As previously mentioned, the *Police Journal* was devoted to 'the police forces of the empire' and a typical issue, such as the one for 1937, includes a list of appointments to Malaya, Hong Kong, Barbados, Northern Rhodesia, the Gold Coast, Uganda and Tanganyika. The list includes five probationers as well as a number of senior officers and commissioners.

A principal source of information on the various structures and functions of the police forces in the outposts of empire are the gazetteers. Again, in the case of India, *The Imperial Gazetteer of India*, published by the Oxford University Press, contains solid information in this respect, as in the volume for 1909 which includes an account of the senior staff, mentioning for example in one district an inspector general, his deputy, a district superintendent and others. As the gazetteer notes: 'The controlling staff is composed almost entirely of Europeans. Recruitment has hitherto been partly by open competition in England, partly by examination after nomination in India, and partly by promotion of subordinate officers.'

Surprisingly, as the gazetteer points out, the template for India was from Ireland: 'The most interesting feature of the modern Indian Police system is that, along with a regular police formed on the model of the Royal Irish Constabulary, it comprises as an essential part of its organisation the ancient institution of the village watch.'

The first step in researching the members of these forces is to look at the National Archives POL series: CO has records of the Colonial Office, Commonwealth and Foreign Office, Empire Marketing Board and other organisations. CO 1037 has the registered files of police recruitment and related material. CO 1037/185 is particularly useful, having lists of pensions of colonial police officers recruited from United Kingdom police forces in 1960. It is an open document. Also within the CO 1037 series is material on the conference of commissioners of police for 1960.

Once again special mention must be made of obituaries or retirement notices, as carried in the *Police Journal* and elsewhere, such as that for the retirement of Sir Henry Dowbiggin, retiring from the position of Inspector-General of Ceylon Police in 1937. If your ancestor was a senior officer, such journal announcements are an excellent source of biographical detail. In that feature, for instance, we learn that Dowbiggin began his career in 1901, putting in 36 years of service in Ceylon. In the course of writing on Dowbiggin's life, the writer also gives a summary of the development of the Ceylon force, in both social and organisational terms.

A pattern will doubtless emerge as you look into all the additional sources. As with so many professions and occupations, the general expectations of the researcher may sometimes be met, but only rarely does a research trajectory move smoothly from source to source, each step amplifying the basic career details found in the staff record, with warrant number, dates of service and promotions. What also becomes clear from the multiplicity of police forces and their resources is that few people in earlier times gave any thought to the future need for organisation and consistency in these records. Prison service records have been similarly limited in this way, with government directives giving prison governors the power to decide whether to preserve or destroy their records.

Chapter 8

NON-GEOGRAPHIC FORCES

The Transport Police

This chapter is devoted to what are sometimes called 'non-Home Office forces' – in other words, those forces that have no geographic location or designated area. This covers transport police and the police responsible for dockyards and similar security work. They largely cover such locations as markets, parks, canals and airports. By far the best established is the Transport Police, whose history stretches back to the years before the founding of the Metropolitan Police. In fact, the police system as we know it today owes a great deal to Sir Patrick Colquhoun, the man whose work led to the formation of the Thames River Police; he published a book in 1796 called *The Police of the Metropolis*. His extensive, far-seeing plans resulted only in a single river patrol, in spite of the fact that he had anticipated most of the new structures that were to follow in the Victorian period.

Regarding transport, however, there was legislation concerning the railways well before the first railway services in the 1830s. Locomotives had been used in collieries and for short journeys linked to industry for around sixty years before the famous Rainhill Trails and the opening of the Liverpool to Manchester Railway in 1830. By this time a police force had been established to protect the line and control the communications involved. As early as 1833 a publication called *The Railway Companion* refers to station houses at every mile along a route. Obviously, as the gangs of navvies came into the country to build the railway network, the police had to supervise them and to combat the disorder that went with drunkenness. At times matters were so out of hand that the army had to be called in.

But naturally, as the railways became a prominent part of everyday life in Victorian times, the Transport Police had to cope with the new crimes that came along with the new industry. Theft of property and from passengers was common. The 1856 Constabulary Act clearly had some effect on the Railway Police, and there was a certain degree of decline in the ranks after that, but in 1900 many of the major rail companies thought again about their own police and organised the forces afresh. For instance, dog patrols were used on night duty to combat pilfering from freight carriages and to catch tramps sleeping where they should not have been.

The First World War had an impact on all transport policing, of course, notably at the docks but also on the railways, both of which were often

LNER detectives at Kings Cross. On the right is DC Herbert ('Bert') Hinchley. A keen photographer of railways, he rose to be Chief Inspector and worked after retirement as Head of Security at Marylebone. His wife was the first policewoman constable on the LNER Police. (Dr John Bond)

targets for the bombers, of course. But there were significant advances, such as the first women police officers being employed (in 1914). Then in 1919 the Railway Police Federation came into being, and a further streamlining of the force was initiated when the 1921 Railway Act amalgamated several small lines. As time went on, training was shared with the regular police forces, and of course during the Second World War the normal scale of crime on the railways accelerated and the force's task was much tougher.

The nature of the force was rationalised during the Second World War and such matters as training and working conditions were attended to; in 1948 the railways across the land were unified and so the police force changed in step with that. In 1962 the British Transport Commission was abolished and the force became simply the British Transport Police. Then in 1992 there was a further reorganisation when the force was split into eight areas, each under the control of an area commander. As historian Kevin Gordon has pointed out, such major developments as the Channel Tunnel have meant that once again the force has had to adapt and change, creating specialised units for the new work that comes along.

There are some records at the force archives, and there is an on-going appeal on the British Transport Police website for donations of all kinds. These archives comprise record cards, photographs, journals, annual reports from chief constables, police manuals, warrant cards and all kinds of personal documents. But the National Archives have most material.

For the earlier period of railway history you will need to search the papers of specific companies, and the first step at the National Archives is to search with the keywords 'police' or 'rail.' The department code AN will take the researcher to records dating to after 1921. AN 2 and AN 3 cover the Second World War (when obviously there was far more going on). In addition, there are the minutes of the Chiefs of Police Committee at AN 3/45 covering those war years, and then AN 97, AN 109 and AN 167 for later years.

There are also a number of items such as rule books, regulations and journals relating to the force, and the only way to find out whether these miscellaneous records are useful to you is to look at the summary entries for contents. So, for instance, it would be worth looking at railway police items under MEPO, HO (Home Office) and MT. Examples include the papers of Inspector James Smith of the North Eastern Railway, covering the years 1888–1915, and in Access to Archives the papers of Edward

This 1937 advertisement for the Motor Bandit Bomb reflects the way policing had changed. (Author's collection)

A sign of the times: increasing numbers of mobile police in 1939. (The Times)

EDUCATING ROAD USERS

800 MORE MOBILE POLICE

Sir John Simon, the Home Secretary, announced in the House of Commons yesterday that it is proposed, as an experiment, to augment the number of police road patrols by about 800 men, not so much with a view to more frequent penal action, but primarily for the purpose of inculcating a higher standard of road sense and behaviour on the part of all classes of road users, including cyclists and pedestrians.

It is understood (our Parliamentary Correspondent writes) that the new scheme will begin in two experimental areas, one in the North of England and the other in the South. The police to be employed will be specially trained, and it may be possible to make use of the special training facilities available for the Metropolitan Police at Hendon. For the experimental period it is proposed to quadruple the present motor patrol strength in the areas selected. The scheme cannot be put into operation until recruits have been appointed and trained to take

Adams of the NER Docks Police: he was a long-serving constable, his dates being 1896–1957.

For staff records the National Archives is not the main source, as the British Transport Police archives have most staff records, and these reach back as far as the 1860s, and there are also useful lists of names of those officers who won gallantry awards (the King's Police Medal). These are all listed in a volume by Peter Farmery, *Police Gallantry: The King's Police Medal, the King's Police and Fire Service Medal and the Queen's Police Medal for Gallantry, 1909–1978*, published in 1995.

Other Specialist Forces

Various constabularies come under the control of local authorities or sometimes of private companies. Acts of Parliament created them for very closely defined responsibilities such as docks and harbours; one such body is the Mersey Tunnel Police. Since they have no police authority, they have to be in close touch with the territorial force in their area. They may be found almost anywhere, from the York Minster Police to the Birmingham Markets Police.

A new type of patrol boat off Wapping. (Author's collection)

Tracing ancestors in these forces requires a trawl through a succession of minor records and ephemera, and indeed extensive use of the internet. For instance, the chat room of RootsChat.com often has enquiries regarding docks employees. However, there are many organisations devoted to the dissemination of knowledge about these localised forces. For instance, the Tees and Hartlepool Harbour Force, consisting of around a dozen officers, had the same uniform and the same equipment as the Cleveland Police, and indeed the same powers – but only within a mile of the land covered by the docks' owners.

The Port of London Police may be traced back to the watchmen employed by individual dock companies back in the eighteenth century; only as the docks were expanded in the nineteenth century was a central authority established to administer the docks. The Tilbury Docks, completed in 1896, are some 26 miles from London, so it makes sense for them to have their own vigilant police force. After the Port of London Authority came into being in 1908, it had its own force, the PLA Police Force. The officers functioned in the same way as the Metropolitan Police, having only a different badge.

The Thames Police launch Vigilant. (Author's collection)

To begin tracing PLA police ancestors, the first step is to contact the archivist at the Port of Tilbury Police, Police Headquarters, Tilbury Freeport, Tilbury, Essex RM18 7DU.

Case Study: The Thames Police, *c.* 1890

In 1955 Detective Inspector David Nixon, known as 'Nick of the River', wrote his memoirs. He was fond of writing about himself in the third person, and at one point explained the beginnings of the Thames Division of the police, linking the marine force of the early nineteenth century to the PLA force a century later, and placing his own Metropolitan division within that network. He described the state of affairs in 1932:

> Five main bodies controlled the river. The River Police of the Thames Division, together with their attached Criminal Investigation Department . . . Then came the Port of London Authority, a government-sponsored body . . . it employed its own private police force. The third body was the Customs and Excise.

Thames Police going on duty, 1891. (*Strand* Magazine)

Inspector Nixon's memoirs are invaluable for the family historian, as he gives a great deal of social history and background. When we know what the ancestor did on a daily basis, we have a greater chance of learning where, why and how various items of documentation fit into the pattern of his life. The resulting image is like a jigsaw, and we place the pieces in carefully, one at a time.

For that reason, contemporary writing is very useful. For example, an intrepid reporter for the *Strand* magazine in 1890 went to spend a night with the Thames Police. He explained the river police's strength at that time: 'Now they are a body of two hundred and two strong, possessing twenty-eight police galleys and a trio of steam launches.' He then goes to Wapping: 'In High Street, Wapping, famous for its river romances and within five hundred yards of the Old Stairs, the principal station of the Thames Police is to be found. The traditional blue lamp projects over a somewhat gloomy passage leading down to a riverside landing-stage.'

Here the reporter meets the staff. He tells his readers, 'These river police know every man who has any business on the water at night.' He then explains their methods of deployment: 'Our little craft has a lively time amongst the fire-floats – for fires are just as likely to occur on the river as on land – and accordingly small launches are dotted about here and there . . . a red light signifies their whereabouts. If the police saw flames, they would do exactly as they do on land.'

In Wapping the reporter met a senior officer, Inspector Fletcher. Inside the station, he noted that 'accommodation is provided for six single men, with a library, reading room, and billiard room at their disposal'. He sketched Inspector Fletcher at his desk, looking solemn, firm and very much in command.

Overall, we learn a great deal about the Thames Police through this early piece of documentary evidence.

*Inspector Fletcher on duty with the Thames Police. (*Strand* Magazine)*

Chapter 9

PROFESSIONAL JOURNALS AND PERIODICALS

Magazines and Periodicals in General

A recurrent theme throughout this book has been the fragmentary nature of the sources for police ancestry. At the basis of this situation is the haphazard and piecemeal state of the records across the various constabularies as they have developed into their present form. The general tendency has been for staff records above and beyond record cards and warrant number lists to be almost entirely without shape or system across the country, and as new constabularies were formed and old ones abandoned, the situation became even more difficult for the modern researcher.

Against such a chaotic background, ephemera and odd documents come into the reckoning, and certainly the numerous police journals have to be counted as valuable. Their usefulness varies markedly, depending on their content. But as previously mentioned with regard to the *Police Gazette*, persistence will generally be rewarded and some mention will be found of a large proportion of officers. For instance, the *Police Journal* throughout the 1920s and 1930s listed appointments to the colonial police, as in this extract from December 1937:

Ellis, J.A. (British Section, Palestine Police)

King, W.C.C. (Chief Commandant of Prisons and Inspector of Police, Cyprus)

Rippon, E.M. (Assistant Inspector of Police, Tanganyika)

But generally, it is difficult to say where might lie the use of such publications for the family historian. In 1991 L.A. Waters wrote a booklet for the Police History Society on this subject and very helpfully surveyed most of the police journals, ranging from about 1830 to the present day. They are all in the index of the British Library Newspaper Library at Colindale Avenue. Full details are given in the Bibliography.

The *Police Gazette* has already been discussed and it has been pointed out that few names appear in it. The appeal of these publications is that by sheer serendipity the name you want will appear in some context, possibly in letters, sports references, honours and so on. But others, with very different agendas, may offer more substance. For instance, *On and Off Duty* was a magazine for the Christian Policemen's Association, running from 1883 to around 1920, and this does contain such items as obituaries. There is also a series of accounts of notable achievements and acts of bravery, along with a feature called 'Flashes from the Forces'. *On and Off Duty* was published in London, initially from Aldersgate Street and later from The Strand.

The *Police Service Advertiser* existed from 1866 to 1959, although it changed its title several times along the way. It was originally a supporter of conditions of service and ran campaigns along those lines, as of course the first agitation for the better arrangement of pensions was taking place early in the journal's history. Some of the features are particularly useful for the family history researcher, notably the annual reports from chief constables and the letters column, and it was also linked to the Police Mutual Assurance Association. From 1866 it printed obituaries of officers who were members of that body, and so provides a useful source for family historians. It even carried subscription lists from the stations from which death benefits would be paid. But the main reason why this is a particularly useful publication is its articles on welfare issues and the biographies in the obituaries.

The *Policewomen's Review* existed from 1927 to 1937 and was published by what was then the Women's Auxiliary Service, later the Women's Police Service. This is extremely valuable for family history, as it carried details of women officers and even had numbers of photographs, usually pictures of women who had just joined specific constabularies.

Special mention must be made of the *Journal of the Police History Society*, currently edited by Chris Forester and printed annually. This has a very wide remit, covering murder stories of officers, police history in all regions, accounts of officers from the past, obituaries, features on little-known forces and of course it has photographs and reviews. For the family historian, it may be useful to summarise the main contents of a sample issue. In 2007, for instance, issue no. 22 contained articles on:

Irish Revenue Police

Cambridge Borough City Police in the Post War Years

Police in Cyprus

The Murder of a Lincolnshire Policeman

Policing Denbighshire, 1800–1850

Correspondence of the Blackburn Watch Committee

Perhaps most useful, in the back numbers, are the features on particular constabularies, as these often have statistics and extracts from the kinds of records found in the county record offices. For example, there may be features on pension schemes and conditions of service.

The *Police Journal*

As has been mentioned previously, this publication was styled 'a quarterly review for the police forces of the empire' but in fact the material included was very wide-ranging and a typical issue carried updates on criminal law, crime writing on notorious cases, forensic studies, explanations of the criminal legal system, research reports and, of course, practical topics such as traffic lights and police boxes. Where it becomes useful to the family historian is in the correspondence, obituaries, biographical notices and listings of colonial appointments.

The lists of appointments have been already discussed, along with the biographical notices. In terms of correspondence, a typical example is a letter about learning Morse Code from Constable Frank Mackie of the Stirling County Constabulary, published in 1937. Many officers took part in the annual King's Gold Medal Essay Competition, such as a piece on traffic problems by R.P. Wilson, Chief Constable of the West Sussex Constabulary. In 1936 there were five recipients of this award, or who were 'commended'; as well as R.P. Wilson, they were F.T. Tarry of Exeter, W.A. Bourne Price of Bengal, Arthur Cain, a sergeant in the Metropolitan Police, and R.J. Preston, a Salford constable.

Of all the publications that are likely to offer names and events across the country, this journal is arguably the best.

Please hand this to a colleague.

THE POLICE JOURNAL.

The SERVICE Journal of the Police Forces.

(N.B.—Supplied only to police officers. It is not available to the public.)

POLICE Officers in every quarter of the globe are readers of *The Police Journal*. Are you one of them ?

This quarterly review is indispensable to all those connected with police work and the administration of the law. No matter what your rank or department may be, the range of subjects covered by *The Police Journal* is so varied that no ambitious officer can possibly afford to neglect it. The Journal contains :

(1) Notes on Recent Crime, from the police point of view.

(2) Notes on Police and the Law, and Police and Public, with reference to recent legal cases and events of importance to policemen.

(3) Recent Judicial, Magisterial and Appeal Court Decisions.

(4) Accounts of serious crimes, describing in detail the police procedure, and steps taken in detection.

(5) Technical articles on photography for policemen, wireless, finger-prints, footprints, chemical tests, etc. These are written in as simple language as possible, difficult technical terms being avoided.

(6) A series of instructional articles, by Prof. F. G. Tryhorn, on the scientific detection of crime, emphasizing the " points " which are of primary importance to " the man on the beat ". These also are written in as simple language as possible.

In addition there are articles dealing with :

(7) The latest mechanical contrivances for the detection of crime.

(8) Cases of ingenious original work by individual policemen deserving of " honourable mention ".

(9) Notes on interesting and instructive police work from the various forces.

(10) Correspondence.

A subscription to *The Police Journal* is an investment !
And the Journal costs 1/6 a quarter !

[P.T.O.]

The Police Journal *calls for contributions, 1937.* (Author's collection)

The *Police Review*

This journal started its life in a context of polemic and dissent, as it was tied up with issues related to working conditions in the police, and more profoundly it was also concerned with esteem, justice and individual rights within the profession. The man who started the publication was John Kempster in 1893, when it was called *Police Review and Parade Gossip*. In many ways it was a groundbreaking enterprise; the rationale was to put up issues for debate and to take a stand on the key subjects of dismissal, working hours, pensions and so on.

A typical *Review* campaign was that in 1907 for Inspector George Groves, who was insisting that he had been unfairly dismissed from Monmouthshire Constabulary. The editor himself spoke out at meetings on Groves' behalf. His offence was to ask a man to give him the money back for the cost of a postage stamp – one penny, in fact. Kempster also formed the Police and Citizen's Association, which did largely what the present-day *Review* does: provide educational materials for promotion exams.

But the *Review*'s main concern was with working conditions, and a typical example was the notion of a police rest-day. This letter was written to *The Times* in 1910, indicating that the *Review* was having an impact:

> Sir, Allow me to support the editor of the *Police Review* in his contention that one day's rest in seven should be given to the constabulary forces of the country. Whether it be true or not that the members of the police force are demanding this reasonable concession appears to me to be beside the mark. The question is surely whether it is in the interest of public policy for any body of workers to be continually employed . . . The policemen employed in our museums and elsewhere on Sundays, in the interest of public order, should have their vacation on another day . . .

Regional battles were also fought, as in the case of Liverpool City Council in 1908; the council had refused to grant constables a pay rise of 2 shillings a week after they had completed fifteen years' service. The cost to the council was stated to be £6,700. But the *Police Review* entered the fray with some statistics of its own on inflation, noting that the price of essentials such as coal, tea and bacon had risen sharply. More relevantly, the journal also told Liverpool City Council that it was paying its officers less than their counterparts in Manchester and nearby Bootle. The Liverpool councillors did not budge, but at least the incident proves that the *Review* was active on behalf of the ordinary constable.

The *Metropolitan Police Journal*

This was produced during the 1920s and 1930s, and is probably the most useful professional journal for family historians, as it contains extensive

METROPOLITAN POLICE
COLLEGE
JOURNAL

Vol. V. No. 1   Spring, 1939

The Metropolitan Police Journal. (Author's collection)

lists of names, often related to prizes, awards and sporting achievements. There are also photographs with names, such as a group picture of colonial cadets in the 1937 issue, showing nine men who were destined to go to serve in various parts of Africa.

Award lists are a good source of names, as in this list of merit awards for the Royal Life Saving Society swimming course in 1937:

> Award of Merit: W.G. Addison-Scott, R.H.M. Bailey, D.G. Brown, K.I. Dexter, G. East, E. Everett, S.J. Harvey, J.L.S. Kirby, A.R. Millar, J.C. Nightingale, E.L. Page, G.M. Smailes and E. Solomon.

Also included are reports on all kinds of events with participants, such as the Debating Society, which discussed the notion that 'The Pen is Mightier than the Sword', when those involved were B.C. Fay, T. Bagshawe, T.C. Hankin-Turvin and W.D. Capper. 'After a lively and interesting debate the motion was lost by 34 votes to 22.'

Case Study: Reports and Enquiries

In the on-going search for secondary material to build up the substance of the life of your police ancestor, one source that is often overlooked is the stock of parliamentary papers, many of which contain reports and enquiries on all aspects of life. In the Victorian and regency periods, for instance, it is a simple matter to find the volumes or texts on microfilm at university libraries. As is so often the case, if you know the dates and constabulary of the person involved, then all these secondary materials may turn up something exciting – material of real interest and substance: newspapers, journals, correspondence at local archives and parliamentary papers.

Reports and enquiries usually involved a panel of experts questioning a representative sample of professionals from the subject under review, so the police enquiries meant that inspectors of police, chief constables, superintendents and humble constables would be called to be interviewed.

As an example of the lists and sometimes biographical details potentially to be found in reports, a study of the reports on the police between the 1830s and 1870s reveals such data as lists of witnesses called for questioning, and sometimes their expenses. For the 1875 report on police superannuation funds, for instance, forty officers of all ranks were

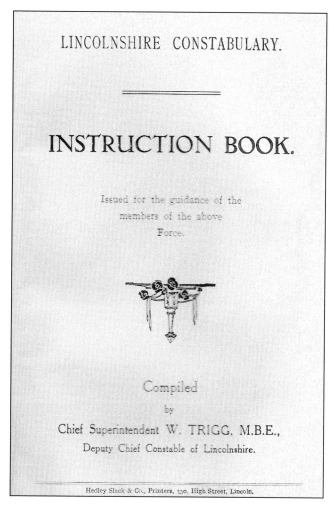

LINCOLNSHIRE CONSTABULARY.

INSTRUCTION BOOK.

Issued for the guidance of the
members of the above
Force.

Compiled
by
Chief Superintendent W. TRIGG, M.B.E.,
Deputy Chief Constable of Lincolnshire.

Hedley Slack & Co., Printers, 330, High Street, Lincoln.

questioned. In most cases, we can read what these witnesses said, as in this summary of the statements made by Robert Brown in 1852:

> Brown, Robert (analysis of his evidence)
>   Superintendent of police in the county of Cumberland, 3030; system of police adopted in the Derwent division; extent of the force and expense thereof; a slight increase in the force would render the police a very efficient body . . . Uselessness of the parish

constables generally – want of co-operation of the police of the towns with those of the Derwent division of the county . . .

The lists of witnesses also appear with the specific dates on which they spoke, as in this section from the report:

Friday 7 May 1875

Mr Robert Hitchman
Mr George Glossop
Captain William Congreve
Colonel Robert Bruce
Mr John Jackson.

Tuesday 11 May 1875

Mr John Dunne
Mr George Lee Fenwick
Mr George Cocksedge
Mr William Stoker
Mr Thomas Fell Molyneux.

Page numbers referring to their testimonies are also given.

Not only do these parliamentary reports give an insight into the attitudes to the police force as it developed, they are also a unique source of information on opinions on important issues. Of course, these reports proliferated during the years of the two important bills of 1838 and 1856, but when superannuation became a hot topic in the profession, enquiries were initiated then as well.

These sessional papers of the House of Commons may be found in county record offices or even in public or university libraries; however, they represent only a portion of the printed documents produced by Parliament over the centuries, and of course they are concerned with debates and discussions following such things as public enquiries. A productive first step before using any of these sources is to consult *A Guide to Parliamentary Papers* by Professor P. and Mrs G. Ford (Blackwell, 1956). Since 1547 there have been journals of the proceedings of the House of Commons; unfortunately most of the original papers were destroyed in the fire of 1834 which burnt down the Houses of

Parliament. But from 1776 the habit of binding papers in volume form began, and in 1803 the so-called Abbot papers began when the Speaker of the House, Charles Abbot, initiated the printing of another collection of 110 bound volumes.

Since 1801 the sessional papers have been grouped under headings of Bills, Reports of Committees, Reports of Commissioners and Accounts and Papers. A sample of the material concerning the police includes a number of items that would be of no use to the family historian, but such items as the Returns of Police Forces 1840–1856 and the Report of the Select Committee on Police Service are clearly of great value.

One writer in 1948, assessing the value of these papers, noted that some correspondence about a young girl called Sarah Chandler of Lincolnshire, who had been sentenced to fourteen days in prison and four years in a reformatory for picking a geranium from a garden, reached the dizzy heights of inclusion in a government white paper. That is why these sources are worth consideration.

Chapter 10

SOME SPECIAL TOPICS

The First Black Police Officer

Former police officer Bob Lowther has researched the history of the Carlisle City Constabulary, and in the process of that project he discovered the life and career of PC John Kent, believed to be the first black police officer in Britain. Kent was born some time around 1795 near Carlisle, the son of one Thomas Kent who worked on the estate of one of the great Cumberland landowners.

Until Kent was discovered, the celebrated officer Norwell Roberts was thought to be the first black officer; Roberts is best known for his part in the film about the arrival of the SS *Windrush* in 1948, bringing the first Caribbean immigrants after the war. He became a detective sergeant in the Metropolitan Police, joining that force in 1966, and won the Queen's Police Medal in 1996.

Bob Lowther uncovered quite a lot of biographical detail about Kent. He found that the officer had been present when a constable was killed in an election riot in 1841, after joining the police as a probationer on 17 August 1837. He was labelled 'a supernumerary constable' on first joining the ranks. In the election riot a crowd had attacked a small force of officers and their chief constable. Kent himself gave evidence at the trial at Carlisle Assizes.

In the obituaries it is recalled that the man was known as 'Black Kent' across the county, and that in the years before he became a policeman he was something of a curiosity, with crowds of people gathering to watch him as he worked on the roads. *The Times* in October 2006 reported that 'he was so well known that a generation of Carlisle children were brought up to fear him'. But there was an ignominious end to his career, as he was dismissed for being drunk on duty, in common with a large proportion of constables in those early years of police history.

In terms of family history, matters will be very different now and in the future: Britain had its first black chief constable in 2003: Mike Fuller of the Kent force. In future research historians will have the services of the National Black Police Association, formed in September 1994 and consolidated after meetings to set up a national communication network in 1996.

Murder Files: Officers Killed on Duty

It has to be said that, given the dangerous nature of police work, there may be a more than average chance that a police ancestor will have met with death or serious injury in the course of his or her duty. Fortunately for the family historian, there is a specialist available to make the details of police deaths known. This is Paul Williams, a former member of the Metropolitan Police, working in their Criminal Record Office. Paul now runs a business called Murder Files, specialising in helping all kinds of historical research into crime history. Paul also used to give talks on the material and stories from the notorious Black Museum of Scotland Yard; he has lectured on the subject to all kinds of visitors, including hangman Albert Pierrepoint. He has stated on his website that he began receiving enquiries from people about their police ancestors and so started to build up a database, and his chronicle of police murders is now available on CD, with the title 'The Ultimate Price: The Unlawful Killing of British Police Officers 1700–1900'.

Some of the early cases are not well documented in the records, and therefore newspaper reports have to be the main source. An example of the kind of material in Paul's CD is the story of Sergeant Winpenny of the West Riding of Yorkshire Constabulary, who was murdered on 23 November 1895 while on duty at Liversedge near Batley. He was beaten to death after trying to arrest a drunken woman. Two people were tried for the offence at the West Riding Quarter Sessions, but they were not charged with his murder. Obviously, this is not the kind of story one wants to find in the family history, but that kind of violent death is naturally not uncommon in the history of policing.

Case studies of researchers finding police deaths in the family history are not hard to find. In the BBC magazine *Who Do You Think You Are?* for

January 2008, we find the story of Judy Rouse, who found out about her police ancestor, Enos Molden, a village constable from Wiltshire who died tragically on 9 April 1892, only a few months before his retirement. Unusually, the essence of the sad story is told on the officer's gravestone, so there was a rare first phase of research open to Judy Rouse. Enos was 50 years old and about to retire from duty at Shrewton when a murder was committed by a member of staff at a local lunatic asylum, John Gurd.

In a fit of jealous rage, Gurd had shot dead a man called Henry Richards and had gone on the run. Enos and two other officers went in search of the miscreant after information about his whereabouts was given to the police. During the pursuit poor Enos was shot, wounded in the side, and he cried out, 'Oh dear I'm shot . . . do take hold of me, I'm dying.' He had joined the police when he was just 21, back in 1843. It was a sad end to a long career.

Sport and Recreation

As already mentioned with reference to the *Police Journal*, sport and recreation activities are an obviously profitable opening for finding information about police officers. The basic reason for this is the popularity of sport and physical fitness in the police. There can be no clearer example of this than the participation of the City of London Police in the 1908 Olympics; in the City archives there is a photograph of the tug-of-war team, nine men with an average weight of 17 stones. The names of the men were: Merriman, Shepherd, Mills, Ireton, Goodfellow, Humphreys, Barrett, Duke (the captain) and Hirons. The records (as held at Wood Street) give biographies of the men, as in this information on Frederick Merriman:

Albert Oldman of the City of London Police, boxing gold medallist. (City of London Archives)

Frederick was born in Gloucestershire. Like his father, he became a tree feller – good training, perhaps, for his chosen sport. He joined the City Police in 1896, aged 22 years, and was recorded as being 5 feet 11 inches tall. Frederick was one of a number of the tug-of-war team to receive a Commendation for skilled first aid, and to end his service at Moor Lane. He retired on pension in 1921 and died aged 67 years in 1940.

The 1908 Olympics were the first at which the gold, silver and bronze medals were awarded; it was also the event which first defined the marathon course at 26 miles and 385 yards, apparently because Princess Mary wished to watch the start of the race from her room in Windsor Castle. The City Police won medals in three sports: tug-of-war, heavy-weight boxing and wrestling. There were three teams taking part for Britain in the tug-of-war: the other two teams were also police teams, one from Liverpool and one from the Metropolitan Police K Division.

The City of London Police rugby football team, 1935/6. (City of London Archives)

Generally, it is not a difficult task for the researcher to find the names of officers involved in major sporting activities: The Times Digital Archive has most of these listings. From there, it is very common to find, at local and regional level, sports event listings of all kinds. For instance, sporting achievements will be recorded in many individual files and cuttings collections. In fact, there is a general trend for constabularies to have collections of magazines and trophies related to sporting achievements in their ephemera.

Genealogy Society Resources

Stating the obvious may sometimes be a valuable thing to do. In this case it is to point out to researchers that experts on genealogy are clearly going to be of use to family history detective work. At the centre of this in Britain is the Society of Genealogists, which offers research material, help and guidance for historians, and publications. They publish a journal, and have also produced a series of booklets, including Anthony Shearman's *My Ancestor was a Policeman*. (The address of their online catalogue is given in the website section in Chapter 12.) Their library has a huge collection of family history titles, and also contains over 9,000 county sources, covering such material as directories, poll books, parish registers and so on. The Society also has a programme of lectures and courses on the subject.

All the Society's publications are available from 14 Charterhouse Buildings, Goswell Road, London EC1M 7BA. As the Society announces on its website: 'Anyone conducting research into family history, social history or biography should benefit from the Society's resources. All our facilities and events are available to members and non-members alike, but members have free access to the library.'

The Scottish Genealogy Society, based in Edinburgh, has some remarkably useful resources for police family history, notably in its monographs. For instance, Peter Ruthven-Murray's *The Edinburgh Police Register, 1815–1859*, which was published in 1991, contains listings of all constables with warrant numbers, dates of joining the force and details of any special events. Peter Ruthven-Murray notes that there is a caveat: 'Users of the register should bear in mind that the high incidence of dismissals from the force may be accounted for by the fact that those members who wanted to resign and were unable to give the required one month's notice . . . would be entered in the register as "dismissed" and forfeit all pay due to them.'

This is an extremely valuable publication, and contains occasional additional information that might shock the researcher at times, such as the information on William Andrew, who joined the force in 1847. We know that he had black hair, black eyes and a fair complexion; he had been a labourer and was single. On 6 June 1858 he was 'stabbed by maniac' and died as a result.

The Society has a library and family history centre where the following sources are available:

Family histories: The Family History Index

CD-ROM collection

Old parish registers on microfilm

Census information

Ireland has the Irish Genealogical Research Society and the Genealogical Society of Ireland. The former was established in 1936, with the primary aim of rediscovering the material lost in the destruction of the Dublin Public Record Office in 1922. It has a collection of material relating to Irish births, marriages and deaths up to 1864, and publishes an annual journal.

The Genealogical Society of Ireland has material in these categories:

Census index: Dun Laoghaire for 1901 and 1911

Queries published

Miscellaneous life events

Members' interests directory

Policing in Jersey

The Channel Islands Family History Society has a service dealing with research queries, and this is the best option for family historians who have ancestors with Jersey police connections. The society has certificates of births, marriages and deaths from 1842. Jersey archives are at the Jersey Heritage Trust, and there one can find such items as minutes of police meetings, correspondence of States and Honorary Police and incident books.

Policing in the nineteenth century in Jersey centred on the institution of the Royal Court, the only court in the island, and so all categories of crime were handled there, and the organisation called the Honorary Police was in control of the parishes. The real advance in police reform came after 1850 when a meeting and enquiry put in motion steps to re-organise the police force. A document of 1848 had previously suggested the establishment of three paid judges and the creation of a police court. By 1852 the decision to create a police force for St Helier was confirmed and the St Helier Paid Police finally came into existence in 1854.

This force became known as the night watch or 'la garde de nuit', and by 1914 the force had twenty-one officers. The year 1935 saw the intro-duction of a police force across the islands. As the States of Jersey website makes clear, 'As a consequence of these recommendations, in 1935 the States adopted the principle of a professional police force operating on an island-wide basis. The controversy which this generated resulted in the necessary legislation being delayed and it was not introduced until some three years later in 1938.'

Obviously, the German occupation stopped any development beyond that, but at last in 1951 the principle of an island-wide force was properly adopted and in 1960 the force became known as the States of Jersey Police Force (*see* Bibliography).

Chapter 11

THE PRINCIPAL MUSEUMS

English Museums

The various police museums are an extremely useful resource for the family historian, and if we bear in mind the chaotic situation with regard to central records, it is to be celebrated that the major museums do offer some help with family history work. The respective websites generally give the applicant very clear information about what materials might be there and how they may be accessed. The usual approach in terms of running and developing a police museum is to create a combination of heritage facility, display centre and information base. The most enterprising ones are described below.

The **Greater Manchester Police Museum** is at 57a Newton Street and has been in existence since 1981. There is an archive collection dealing with former police officers from the Manchester and Salford districts; there are also some registers from Salford covering the years 1914–1969 and some from Rochdale and Oldham for the period between the 1940s and the 1960s.

The registers give serial numbers, date of entry, surname, first name, nationality and birthplace. In terms of police material, the main categories are:

Constables' reports

Police and crime investigation manuals

The *Police Gazette* on microfilm

The *Police Review*

Press cuttings

Personnel records.

The personnel records cover Bolton, Greater Manchester, Oldham, Rochdale Borough, Rochdale, Salford and Stockport. The years covered vary from force to force, but the most substantial are for Manchester (1858–1975) and Salford (1867–1946).

The **Essex Police Museum** has one of the most extensive and interesting databases available for police history. Here you will find a long list of features on police events and personnel, including some fairly full accounts of such items as police deaths, the King's Police Medal and wartime incidents. For instance, these are some of the items featuring police staff of various ranks and periods:

The Making of a Chief Constable: A former naval officer, John McHardy was the first Chief Constable of Essex. Through his

Manchester Police ambulance service, 1900. (Reproduced by courtesy of the Greater Manchester Police Museum)

experience and guidance his county police force became one of the most efficient in the country.

'The slaying of parish constable Trigg': A most atrocious murder at Berden was that of Henry Trigg in 1814. It took a year to track down the two thieves who had gunned him down.

'The dogged detective: The life and times of David Scott'. Retiring after thirty-seven years of service, this man left behind a legacy of achievements.

The **Ripon Museum Trust** is linked to the Ripon heritage establishment of the police museum and courthouse/gaol. The list of sources, obtainable through the Access to Archives site, shows the diversity of materials available there. Typical items are: a roll of honour book for service personnel killed in the Second World War; a testimonial to a constable at Monkfrystone Hillam; first aid certificates issued to police constables, and so on.

A visit to the museum itself offers one of the most impressive historical heritage experiences related to the social history of policing. It is housed in a building that was formerly the House of Correction and Liberty Gaol; in 1887 the Ripon City Police Force was amalgamated with the West Riding Constabulary, and the old buildings have now been transformed into an integral part of the educational experience of 'stepping back in time' to comprehend the life of a police officer in Victorian times. Displays cover the development of policing from the early medieval period to modern times.

A similar establishment is found at the **Old Police Cells Museum** in the basement of Brighton town hall. This offers visitors the experience of walking into the old police station of what was Brighton Borough Police, where they will 'learn about the murder of Chief Constable Henry Solomon by a prisoner in 1844'. One of the most attractive features for the family historian with links to that area is the extensive photo archive of the force. Once again, the big attraction for the historian is to access borderline secondary material.

The **West Midlands Police Museum** offers sound advice about dealing with many of the frustrating features of police personnel records, as stated so far in the present work, but it also offers friendly help with enquiries. Their website gives users a link to access; the records in question cover all the previous forces which were dissolved before the West Midlands Police came into existence. Records are subject to a seventy-five year closure but records for officers who joined one of the relevant forces prior to 1930 are available. The museum is at Sparkhill and the website is www.westmidlandspolicemuseum.co.uk/information.

The **Hampshire Constabulary** has a History Society and a very informative website. Their police museum is at the Netley Training School, and Hampshire Record Office has an annotated searchable bibliography. The History Society works alongside the County Record Office and they have a notice-board for queries on police ancestry. The website is hchs@hantsweb.org.uk for the Hampshire Constabulary History Society.

Museums in Ireland

The **Garda Siochana Museum**, housed in Dublin Castle, is the museum of the Republic of Ireland's national police force. Therefore its material covers the Irish Constabulary, the Royal Irish Constabulary, the Dublin Police and the Dublin Metropolitan Police. The archives contain Garda publications from 1922 to the present time, along with departmental records. There is a personnel register covering the years from 1836 to the 1970s for the Dublin Metropolitan Police, and there is genealogical material on general family histories related to the relevant forces.

Obviously, this is one institution in which a direct application to the archivist is necessary, and these details are given in the next chapter. There is a definitive historical work on the Garda, which would be very useful for the researcher. This is Gregory Allen's *The Garda Siochana: Policing Independent Ireland 1922–1982* (1999).

For police ancestors in Northern Ireland, there is a much more easily accessible resource. The **Police Museum** in Belfast has microfilm records of the Royal Irish Constabulary for 1822–1922 (though these reproduce what is available at the Public Record Office at Kew). The website states that searches for individuals can be made, for a small charge. The following information can be supplied on officers: number, name, age on joining, height, religion, date of appointment, native county, name of person recommending them for the constabulary, trade on joining, places served, with dates, promotions, awards, punishments, injuries, date of marriage and native county of the wife.

The museum was established in 1983 and a Police Historical Society was also founded for the Royal Ulster Constabulary. The museum has a research facility and an excellent photographic archive. An encouraging tone for present purposes is found in the statement made for the museum on the website regarding family history: 'The Museum . . . receives numerous enquiries from home and abroad from people seeking information about the service records of relatives who have previously served'. Altogether, this is a site that is very receptive to the needs of family researchers. At the heart of it is an enthusiastic group of historians.

Museums in Scotland

The **Glasgow Police Museum** is primarily a museum of social and professional history, with no real emphasis given to family history, but the site does have some interesting personal profiles and biographical material, in particular in the section on detectives. The first Glasgow detective was Peter McKinlay, who was appointed in 1819 and was officially called a 'Criminal officer'. The Detective Department was then created in 1821. The site has accounts of some notable officers who followed in that noble tradition, such as DCS Tom Goodall who joined the force in 1932. He was perhaps best remembered for his investigative work in Lanarkshire in 1958.

Much earlier was Detective Lieutenant Archie Carmichael who joined the Glasgow Police in 1859, and later came to be called 'Glasgow's Sherlock Holmes'. For thirty years he served as a detective, and was a police officer for a total of forty-one years. He died in 1900.

This kind of biographical material is always useful, and at this particular site it is perhaps the most interesting approach for the family historian.

In contrast, **Strathclyde Police Archives** pay more attention to family history. The police archives are kept with the Glasgow City Council Archives and for access and information a visit to the Glasgow City Archives is the first step.

Other forces have websites of only limited usefulness, typified perhaps by the **Tayside Police Museum**, although this does have photographs, medals and correspondence in its collection. Note that the area now covered by Tayside (formed in 1975) previously included the Angus, Dundee City and Perth and Kinross forces. Contact with the curator is the best approach. The website is www.tayside.police.uk/history.

The unification of the modern police force was really brought about by the Royal Commission of 1960, and throughout the years 1964–1973 the process was streamlined. As Martin Stallion and David Wall wrote in their book *The British Police*: 'The Commission proposed to increase the size of forces and reduce the overall number of forces to allow for a more efficient administration at local level . . . The powers of the new police authorities were far inferior to those of their predecessors, particularly in the boroughs . . .'. It was a far-reaching revolution, and it created some difficulties for future historians. In Scotland the implications for the researcher are typified by the Tayside Police collections.

Chapter 12

WEBSITES: A SELECTION AND SURVEY

Naturally, the internet is constantly expanding, and the number of websites can be confusing; also, as historians are fully aware, caution has to be exercised in the use and integration of information from the internet generally. For these reasons I have tried here to organise the mass of information in a meaningful way. I have included most of the general historical sites which tend to contain material on crime, law and order in broad terms, and then follow this by surveying more specific police history sites.

The whole picture here covers official sites, information controlled by enthusiasts and of course commercial sites. I have made sure that all references within the text are included here, and in some cases the following Bibliography contains works which relate to particular societies with websites, as in the Society of Genealogists for example. Lists of police history sites are also here, as the resources of social history often overlap with family history and can provide some surprisingly valuable secondary information at times.

Some of these resources are very specialised, but only by a quick survey can the usefulness to each individual be ascertained, so a comprehensive list seemed to be the most sensible option.

General

www.A2A.org.uk
Access to Archives site.

www.aim25.ac.uk/history/
This is a project in progress, aiming to consolidate access to a large
number of higher education centres in Britain.

www.archon.nationalarchives.gov.uk/archon/
The Archon directory provides contact details for archive repositories.

www.archiveshub.ac.uk
This is a general gateway to open details of access to material in univer-
sities and colleges.

www.bopcris.ac.uk
Bopcris opens up details of British official publications from between
1688 and 1995.

http:/balh.co.uk/
The British Association for Local History has all kinds of resources. Its
journal often has extended articles on police history.

http://www.bl.uk/
The British Library: a gateway to all bibliography.

http://www.bl.uk/catalogues/newspapers.html
This is the British Library newspaper catalogue site.

http://oxforddnb.com/
This is the online *Dictionary of National Biography*. Within these pages,
biographies of major figures in police history will be found, going back
to the first Metropolitan Commissioners, and to Sir Robert Peel himself.

www.channelislandshistory.com/left.asp
On this site can be found the access details for the genealogy and police
records discussed in Chapter 10.

http://www.victorianlondon.org/
The site for the *Dictionary of Victorian London*, this is very informative
with regard to the social history of policing in the city.

www.eastlondonhistory.com
http://eserver.org/18th/
This is the Eighteenth-Century Studies site.

www.eolfhs.org.uk
This is the site for the East of London Family History Society.

http://familysearch.com/
The searchable database contains a massive number of names, all put
together by the Church of Jesus Christ of Latter-day Saints.

http://www.gazettes-online.co.uk/
This covers the gazettes published in London, Belfast and Edinburgh.

http://www.history.ac.gh/
The Guildhall Library: very useful for further searches into the City of
London Police.

www.igrsoc.org/about.html
This is the site for the Irish Genealogical Research Society.

http://www.historicaldirectories.org/
The University of Leicester runs this and it is a good source of local
information from directories covering the years from 1750 to 1919.

http://historynews.chadwyck.com/
This has newspaper sources for the nineteenth and twentieth centuries.

http://www.history.ac.uk/search/welcome
This has over 40,000 records on bibliographical sources, and also a
number of good links.

http:// www.bodley.ox.ac.ukilej/
This is Oxford University's site for access to eighteenth- and nineteenth-
century journals.

http://www.local-history.co.uk/
This is the site for *Local History* magazine.

http://www.nationalarchives.gov.uk
The National Archives site: it leads on to all the other adjoining services
as mentioned in the text, and also to the National Archives Learning
Curve.

http://www.nationalarchives.ie/
This is the site for the National Archives of Ireland, and has material on genealogy and on local history.

http://www.nas.gov.uk
This is the counterpart of the above site for Scotland.

http://c19.chadwyck.co.uk
This is part of the massive Chadwyck Healey reference resource network, and contains a wide selection of printed works from the nineteenth century, including some on the subject of crime and law.

http://www.oldbaileyonline.org/
The Old Bailey records contain material accounts of over 100,000 criminal trials at the Central Criminal Court, covering the years from 1674 to 1834.

http://oralhistory.org.uk
This is the oral history site run by the University of Essex.

http://www.rhs.ac.uk/bibl/
This is the site for the Royal Historical Society. The main attraction is the massive bibliography, parts of which cover every aspect of crime and law.

http://www.victoriantimes.org/
This has extensive material on the Victorian period.

Police History and Records

These sites are specifically related to police history, mostly the ones mentioned in the text. Also included are the various museums and sites run by specialists with particular interests. The guide to police archives is the fundamentally important one for tracing police ancestry. This was compiled by Martin Stallion and is now part of Professor Clive Emsley's resource centre at the Open University. It is available at www.open. ac.uk/Arts/history/policing/police-archives-guide/index.html and, as discussed in the first chapter, has listings of the holdings of all repositories, from museums to archives, across the country. It was first assembled for the Police History Society.

Sometimes the police had to deal with delicate, political work: police handling a suffragette protest. (Author)

www.policehistory.com

This is a site for police history in Ireland. The police force in Ireland goes back to the 1814 Peace Preservation Act and by the middle of the nineteenth century the manpower was around 9,000 men. Here you will find materials on the Garda Siochana as described in the previous chapter.

www.policememorial.org.uk

This listing is a full record of all officers from forces in the United Kingdom who lost their lives on duty. This is a roll, to be supplemented by Paul Williams' facility at Murder Files (discussed in Chapter 10). But the value of this is that it is possible to search by regional force names. It is augmented by the Gallantry Roll, a list of sixty-eight posthumous awards made since 1909.

www.blacksheepindex.co.ukPOLNOTES.htm

This is an invaluable resource for tracing police ancestors: amazingly, it provides references to newspaper reports covering the years 1850 to 1920, with the focus on the names of 60,000 police officers. For instance, here are two entries:

Abbott, Thomas, Inspector City Police, blinded by wife, 1900

Cook, Charles Henry, Essex, Biography and photo, 1896

For a small fee, the press accounts may be accessed via the Acrobat reader.

www.btp.police.uk
This is the site of the British Transport Police, and it provides a very detailed historical timeline, with plenty of names of personnel along the way, from the first woman officer to those involved in major incidents.

www.chartists.net
This is the site dealing with Chartist history, and since the police were involved in controlling Chartist activities from the beginning as the movement for parliamentary reform gathered pace, there are records of the police officers involved. For instance, the Metropolitan Police officers in Birmingham ordered to be vigilant in watching the Chartist Convention of 1838 are listed. Superintendents received £17 for this work. The names can also be accessed at the National Archives as MEPO 1/63. On that list there are two superintendents, one sergeant and twenty-five constables.

www.cityoflondonpolicehistory.info
This site has recently been put together by Peter Rowe of the Police History Society.

www.devon-cornwall.police.uk/v3/about/history
This is an historical site, with features on the social history of policing generally and also in that region specifically.

www.empiremuseum.co.uk
This is the site for the Bristol museum at which records of the Palestine Police Force are held.

www.essex.police.uk/museum/history
This is the site with the extensive resource of biographical entries and news stories from the past featuring Essex officers. It is possible to order copies of their 'History Notebook' series and also to order a free copy of a History Notebook general publication on Essex police history.

www.wyevalley.worldonline.co.uk
This is the site for the Palestine Police Old Comrades' Association, based in Nottingham.

Silver salver presented to the force surgeon, George Burlase Childs, by the officers, sergeants and constables of the City of London Police 'as a mark of their esteem and appreciation of his great kindness and professional skill on his retirement as Surgeon to the Force after 41 years of service, on 29 June 1885'. Mr Childs was born on 7 July 1816 and died on 8 November 1888. (City of London Archives)

www.gmp.police.uk/mainsite/pafges/history.htm
The Greater Manchester Police site has the registers discussed in Chapter 11.

www.met.police.uk/information/historical_enquiries.htm
This is the site dealing with records management for the Metropolitan Police.

www.murderfiles.com
This is Paul Williams' site devoted to crime research. Enquiries on
police deaths in history, and orders for the CD-ROM with the
biographies of police officers killed in the execution of their duty may
be sent to enquiry@murderfiles.com.

http://nepolicehistory.homestead.com
This is the site for the North-Eastern Police History Society.

www.oldpolicecellsmuseum.org.uk
This is the museum at Brighton, discussed in Chapter 11.

www.policehistorysociety.co.uk
This is the most significant historical resource available, with a large
number of links.

www.psni.police.uk/index
This site for the Police Service of Northern Ireland has an extensive
range of historical material, and offers family history tracing for a small
fee. The details outlined in Chapter 11 may be accessed for a fee of £15
(in 2008).

www.policemuseum.org.uk
This is the Glasgow Police Museum site, and it proudly announces that
it is the site for the first police force in the United Kingdom. Mainly
providing social history, the museum does have several useful links.

www.riponmuseums.co.uk/html/prison.html
The Ripon museum site has lots of police social history. But note also
that the related holdings as listed in Access to Archives (A2A) give a
fuller picture of what resources and materials are available in Ripon.

www.strathclyde.police.uk/index
This Strathclyde site has useful advice on tracing police ancestors and
gives contact details for help with enquiries. This is also the one which
gives profiles of former detectives in the force.

www.surreymuseums.org.uk/museums
This is the site for the Surrey Police Museum.

www.tayside.police.uk/history
This Tayside site is useful for social history in the area, and notably for
force photographs.

www.westmidlandspolicemuseum.co.uk/information
The West Midlands Police have recently added a special service to their
site, found at www.staffordshire.go.uk/leisure/archives/Online
Catalogues/StaffordshirePoliceIndex.htm, which gives a complete
online index to the county force registers: the staff records for everyone
serving in the years between 1842 and 1977. If your ancestor is located
in the index, a full transcript may be ordered. This material would
include the kind of information discussed in Chapters 2 and 3.
Currently (2008) the cost of this transcript is £5 +p&p.

The Police History Society Publications

The Police History Society is a useful point of reference for family historians for many reasons. It publishes a journal and a newsletter, and these
publications contain a wealth of information on all aspects of police
history. The Society members have varied research interests, and the
features often reflect this. While the journal tends to include items on
individuals and on historical topics, the newsletter often updates readers
on current research interests and on new developments. For instance,
members often write monographs on particular forces, often those which
became defunct many years ago.

A typical feature of special interest in the present context is found in
the newsletter for 2005, in which Edith Smith, the first policewoman, is
remembered, with reference to a feature on her life in an information
sheet produced by Grantham Museum. Edith began her police career in
Grantham in August 1915, being appointed by the Watch Committee.
She left the constabulary in January 1918 because of ill health. As the
information sheet says of her:

> Edith Smith single-handedly cleaned up the town, the theatres and
> the picture houses, which were previously happy hunting grounds
> for prostitutes. In addition, she carried out prisoner escort duties,
> supervised female searches, took sex offence statements, acted as a
> probation officer for many young girls and generally helped
> women in need.

The Society is perhaps most succinctly defined as a source of information
for the social history of the police, and that covers anything from the
nature of uniforms and weapons to the careers of constables and even

The hypothetical case opens. " X " is taken to the " body " of a victim of a hit-and-run driver. " X " questions a witness, who describes a car which passed at the time. Unfortunately the man failed to observe its number.

This detective training scene is from a documentary record of the special detective training programme established in the 1930s. This was produced by Percy Hoskins, who was crime reporter for the Daily Express. (Author's collection)

such topics as forensics and statistics on crime and law from years gone by. In 1987 L.A. Waters, writing a guide to police ancestry, remarked that many researchers believe the Society to be an organisation whose principal aim is resourcing ancestry research. The statement made then applies just as much today: Les Waters wrote, 'Many such family historians found that they were unable to obtain information to help with their research . . . and I began to receive a steady trickle of letters seeking pointers to new sources'. The notion of 'new sources' gets to the heart of the problem. Research on an individual officer may soon peter out after a few basic facts; after that it is a matter of persistence. The Society does not, of course, exist to aid the quest for a police ancestor, but it can provide contacts if a researcher has run out of historical avenues to pursue.

BIBLIOGRAPHY

L isted here are all the publications referred to in the text, along with major reference works, journal articles and material relating to the social history of policing. The publications dealing directly with police ancestry are often scattered across a range of journals and magazines, and the subject is one that attracts a number of related interests, and so it is recommended that you take a look at the indexes of the family history magazines *Ancestors, Family History, Who Do You Think You Are?* and *Practical Family History*.

I have also included a survey of monographs and memoirs by former police personnel, and although these are mostly out of print the second-hand specialist crime history/true crime booksellers all issue catalogues or have searchable websites. These booksellers are:

Bolland Books, e-mail info@bollandbooks.com

Clifford Elmer Books, www.truecrime.co.uk

Loretta Lay Books, www.laybooks.com

Undercover Books, www.clique.co.uk/member/undercover

Also extremely useful is the Bibliography of British Police History, a database created by Stanley Nash of Rutgers University Library, and now also updated by the Open University. In this you may search by author and title, as well as by publication date, historical period or item type. Go to http://www.open.ac.uk/Arts/policebiblio/search.cfm.

Reference

In general, for broad accounts and listings of principal officers, check civic directories, Whitakers Almanac and general trade directories. The *Police Almanac*, as already discussed, has this information (for senior officers) in most depth.

Carter, Paul and Thompson, Kate, *Sources for Local Historians* (Phillimore, 2005)

Cook, Chris, *The Routledge Companion to Britain in the Nineteenth Century* (Routledge, 2005)

Cyriax, Oliver, *The Penguin Encyclopedia of Crime* (Penguin, 1996)

Dell, Simon, *The Victorian Policeman* (Shire Publications, 2004)

Fido, Martin and Skinner, Keith, *The Official Encyclopedia of Scotland Yard* (Virgin Publishing, 1999)

Friar, Stephen, *The Sutton Companion to Local History* (Sutton, 2001)

Hickey, D.J. and Doherty, J.E.A., *New Dictionary of Irish History from 1800* (Gill & Macmillan, 2005)

Johnson, Charles, *The Public Record Office* (SPCK/Macmillan, 1948)

Kuhlicke, F.W. and Emmison, F.G., *English Local History Handlist* (Historical Association, 1965)

Pearsall, Mark, *The National Archives Family History Companion* (National Archives, 2007)

Powell, W.R., *Local History from Blue Books* (Historical Association Handlist, 1948)

Scott, Sir Harold (ed.), *The Concise Encyclopedia of Crime and Criminals* (Rainbird, McClean, 1961)

Stallion, Martin and Wall, David S., *The British Police: Police Forces and Chief Officers, 1829–2000* (Police History Society, 1999)

Police Ancestry

Blatchford, Robert (ed.), *The Family and Local History Handbook* (Robert Blatchford Publishing, York, produced annually)

Gendocs: Genealogical research in England and Wales: this site has a useful section on Victorian London research and the London Police Divisions. *See* http://homepage.ntlworld.Com/hitch/gendocs/police

Shearman, Anthony, *My Ancestor was a Policeman* (Society of Genealogists Publications, 2002)

Waters, L.A., *Notes for Family Historians* (Police History Society, 1987, Police History Monographs no. 1)

Police History: General

Cobb, Belton, *Critical Years at the Yard* (Faber & Faber, 1956)
   Note: this has a listing of police officers and index
Cobb, Belton, *The First Detectives and the early career of Richard Mayne* (Faber, 1957)
Critchley, T.A.A., *History of Police in England and Wales 900–1966* (Constable, 1967)
Donnelly, D. and Scott, K. (eds), *Policing Scotland* (Willan, 2005)
Emsley, Clive, *The English Police: a political and social history* (Pearson Education, 1991)
Farmery, J. Peter, *Police Gallantry: the King's Police Medal, the King's Police and Fire Service Medal and the Queen's Police Medal* (Periter, 1995)
Fitzgerald, Percy, *Chronicles of Bow Street Police Office* (Patterson Smith, 1972)
Harris, Andrew T., *Policing the City: crime and legal authority in London* (Ohio State University, 2000)
Herbert, Barry, *Ticket to the Gallows and other villainous tales from the tracks* (Silver Link, 2002)
Holdaway, Simon (ed.), *The British Police* (Edward Arnold, 1979)
Jones, Steve, *The Illustrated Police News: Victorian court cases and sensational stories* (Wicked Publications, 2002)
Kirby, Dick, *You're Nicked! Further memoirs from the real Sweeney on life in the serious crime squad* (Robinson, 2007)
Lock, Joan, *The British Policewoman, Her Story* (Robert Hale, 1979)
Lock, Joan, *Dreadful Deeds and Awful Murders: Scotland Yard's first Detectives* (Barn Owl Books, 1990)
Moylan, J.F., *Scotland Yard and the Metropolitan Police* (Putnam's, 1929)
O'Connor, Mary T., *On the Beat: a woman's life in the Garda Siochana* (Gill & Macmillan, 2005)
Palmer, Stanley H., *Police and Protest in England and Ireland 1780–1850* (Cambridge University Press, 1988)
Reith, C.A. *Short History of the British Police* (Oxford University Press, 1948)
Selwood, A.V., *Police Strike 1919* (W.H. Allen, 1978)
Stead, Philip (ed.), *Pioneers in Policing* (McGraw Hill, 1977)
Stead, Philip, *The Police of Britain* (Macmillan, 1985)
St Johnston, Sir Eric, *One Policeman's Story* (Barry Rose, 1978)
Taylor, David, *Crime, Policing and Punishment in England 1750–1914* (Macmillan, 1998)

Wade, Stephen, *Plain Clothes and Sleuths: a history of the detective in England* (Tempus, 2007)

Weinberger, Barbara, *The Best Police in the World: An Oral History Of English Policing* (Scholar Press, 1995)

Whitbread, J.R., *The Railway Policeman* (Harrap, 1961)

Palestine and Colonial Police Forces

Angus, John McDonald, *Khaki and Blue: a soldier's and police officer's life 1930–2002* (Athena Press, 2005). This includes a description of his time in the Kenya Police.

Godsave, Jim, 'The Palestine Police', in the *Journal of the Police History Society*, no. 18 (2003), 2–4

Edwards, S.M., *The Bombay City Police: a historical sketch 1672–1916* (Oxford University Press, 1923)

Herbert, Ian, 'The Black Police Officer who Pounded the Beat 150 Years Ago', *The Independent*, Friday, 20 October 2006, p. 28

Horne, Edward, *A Job Well Done* (Anchor Press, 1982)

Imray, Colin, *Policeman in Palestine: memories of the early years* (Edward Gaskell, 1995)

Iver, G.C.B., *In An Indian District* (Civil & Military Gazette 1919)

Jones, Philip, *Britain and Palestine 1914–1948: archival sources for the History of the British Mandate* (Oxford University Press, for the British Academy, 1979)

Lang, Michael, *One Man in his Time: the diary of a Palestine policeman* (Book Guild, 1997)

Morton, Geoffrey J., *Just the Job: some experiences of a colonial policeman* (Hodder & Stoughton, 1957)

Roubicek, Marcel, *Echo of the Bugle: extinct military and constabulary forces in Palestine and Transjordan* (Franciscan Printing Press, 1975)

Rumbelow, Donald, *150 Years of service*. This booklet, first issued in 1989, is on the City of London Police website.

Sinclair, Georgina, *At The End of the Line: colonial policing and the imperial Endgame 1945–1980* (Manchester University Press, 2008)

Police History Society Monographs

1. Waters, L.A., *Notes for Family Historians* (Police History Society, 1987, Police History Monographs no. 1)
2. A Guide to the Archives of Police Forces in England and Wales (see Chapter 2)
3. *The Directory of Police Forces in England and Wales, 1844* (facsimile)
4. *Towards a record management policy*
5. *A History of Chipping Norton Borough Police 1836–1857*

Articles in Journals and Magazines

I have included here only those articles relating to biographical features of family history topics, using representative items from main runs of journals. The Police History Society can supply details from an index.

Adolf, Anthony, 'Law and Order' (Palestine Police), *Practical Family History* (January 2008), 18–21

Anon., 'A Night with the Thames Police', *Strand Magazine* (1891)

Bramham, Peter, 'Policing an Industrial Town: Keighley 1800–1856', *Local Historian* vol. 35, no. 4 (November 2005)

Clements, Dr F., 'Policing in Denbighshire, 1800–1850', *Journal of the Police History Society* no. 22 (2007), 21–24

Feather, Fred, 'Hobby Bobbies', *The Family and Local History Handbook* 9 (Blatchford, 2007), 182–5

Feather, Fred, 'A Police Murder in Hertfordshire', *Journal of the Police History Society* no. 18 (2003), 7–8

Hird, Nicholas, 'From Watchmen to New Police in the Provinces: Huddersfield's Evolutionary Process', *Journal of Regional and Local Studies* vol. 20, no. 2 (Winter, 2000), 28–43

Lock, Joan, 'Grantham's other First Lady', *Journal of the Police History Society* no. 21 (2006), 5–6

Savile, J., 'Policing Chartism 1839–1848. The Role of the Specials Reconsidered', *English Historical Review* vol. CXXII, no. 497

Thomas, Orla, 'Murder on the Beat', *Who Do You Think You Are?* (4 January 2008), 26–8

Regional Force Histories

More and more publications on the histories of various constabularies are appearing all the time, with a plethora of small booklets on particular forces and regions. Some are self-published and some are published by various professional societies or by local history groups. This selection includes some commentaries on typical memoirs as well as a list of force histories. Obtaining some of these items might be difficult, but in most cases they are recent publications, often obtainable by inter-library loan or by order from booksellers (the specialist stockists listed on p. 113 offer a search on request facility). The following titles provide a sample of the local and regional histories available, and obviously they are of special importance to family historians, as many deal with extinct forces and so provide insights into the culture, influences and professional environment the ancestor in question would have experienced.

Anderson, John Eustace, *The Old Mortlake Watch* (R.W. Simpson, Richmond, 1896)

Archibald, T.W.A., *History of the Lothian and Borders Police* (Author, Edinburgh, 1986)

Beazley, Ben, *Peelers to Pandas. An illustrated history of the Leicester City Police* (Breedon Books, 2001)

Clarke, A.A., *Country Coppers. The story of the East Riding Police* (Arton Books, 1993)

Cockcroft, W.R., *From Cutlasses to Computers: The police force in Liverpool 1836–1989* (S.B. Publications, Market Drayton, 1991)

Davey, B.J., *Lawless and Immoral. Policing a Country Town, 1838–1857* (Leicester University Press, 1983). The subject here is Horncastle in Lincolnshire.

Davies, Dewi, *Law and Disorder in Breconshire 1750–1880* (D.G. and A.S. Evans, no date)

Dixon, Brian, *A Very Special Force: 175th Anniversary of Hampshire Special Constabulary* (published by the author, Old Basing Police Station, 54 Bellevue Road, Old Basing RG24 7LG)

East, G.C., *The Constables of Claro: a history of policing in Harrogate and District* (Author, Harrogate, 1996)

Goslin, R.J., *Duty Bound. A history of the Bolton Borough Police Force, 1839–1969* (Bolton Borough Council, 1970)

Grant, Douglas, *The Thin Blue Line. The story of the City of Glasgow Police* (John Long, 1973)

Hann, Maurice, *Policing Victorian Dorset* (Dorset Publishing, 1989)

Hyndman, David, *Nottingham City Police. A pictorial history, 1860–1968* (Davage, 1969)

Madigan, T.J., *The Men Who Wore Straw Helmets. Policing Luton, 1840–1974* (Book Castle, 1993)

Morson, Maurice, *A Force Remembered. The Illustrated History of the Norwich City Police, 1836–1967* (Breedon Books, 2000)

Pringle, Nik and Treversh, Jim, *150 Years Policing in Watford District* (Radley Shaw, 1991)

Reilly, John W., *Policing Birmingham. An account of 150 years of police in Birmingham* (Author, 1990)

Scollan, Maureen, *Sworn to Serve. Police in Essex* (Phillimore, 1993)

Smith, Gordon, *Bradford's Police* (City of Bradford Police, 1974)

Swift, Roger, *Police Reform in Early Victorian York, 1835–1856* (University of York, Borthwick Paper no. 73, 1988)

Taylor, Denis, *999 And All That* (Oldham Corporation, 1968)

Thomas, R.L. (ed.), *Kent Police Centenary, 1857–1957* (Kent Police, 1957)

Turnbull, J.D., *The Ulster Watchdogs* (Aldergrove, 1975)

Waller, Stanley, *Cuffs and Handcuffs. The story of the Rochdale police through the years 1252–1957* (Watch Committee, Rochdale, 1957)

Wood, Dennis, *On The Beat: true tales of a former Manchester Police Officer* (P. and D. Riley, 2005) ISBN 1 874712 77 8

Woodgate, John, *The Essex Police* (Terence Dalton, 1985)

A Survey of Monographs and Memoirs

There is a vast amount of material on police biography and autobiography. Although these publications are usually produced by the author himself or by small local presses, they are worth searching for: after all, a person who has served in the force at the time of your ancestor provides the kind of oral history that is a genuine treasure when you are trying to understand the exact milieu in which the ancestor moved and worked. The following selection is meant to highlight the uses these books have for the family historian.

Again, because some of these publications may not have an ISBN number, the first move is to contact the specialist librarians in the local studies section of the relevant library. Often such police memoirs are found in county magazines also. In my own county, Lincolnshire, for instance, a former constable from Grimsby and Barton on Humber has written a series of articles on his police life for the county magazine supplement. Many of the most recent biographies have been written by commissioners, top detectives and people who moved from police work to something else. Autobiographies of bobbies on the beat are a genre that is being increasingly forced into small-scale publishing, but nevertheless there is much of value to the historian in any literature that has emerged from the region or city in which the ancestor lived and worked.

Fryer, Bert, *Recollections of a Country Copper, 1936–1966* (Author, 1996)
     Fryer served in Lincolnshire, and wrote that in 1936 'The status of the country policeman was fairly high in some quarters, especially in a village. The wages were good, and clothing was provided and also a house.' From books like these the researcher can learn about pay and conditions very quickly. Fryer earned £4 10s a week as a constable. Later he became a member of the CID in Spalding. Therefore we have the course of his career in the book, from dealing with drunken fights to learning about court procedure and studying his force handbook. Several other officers are mentioned throughout the book, and this offers the most value for family historians: the recreation of the station and beat camaraderie, the characters, the crooks and the social context of all the crimes in the spectrum.

Smethurst, Thomas, *A Policeman's Notebook* (Aurora Publishing, no date)
     Smethurst was in the Stalybridge Borough Police for most of his career, but earlier served for a few years with the Bolton Borough Police. His career spans the years from 1888 to the early 1920s. This is mostly a collection of short accounts of every kind of crime we might expect in such an area, from petty theft to suicide and the occasional homicide, but for family history the documentary items such as the 'annual report' are of more interest; he writes, for example: 'The force was inspected by Lieutenant Colonel Eden, His Majesty's Inspector of Constabulary, and the usual certificate of efficiency was received from the Home Secretary . . . The Fire Brigade consists of 1 Chief officer, 1 Second Officer and 18 firemen who with two exceptions are connected with the fire station and police office with call bells.'

Addresses of Organisations

Police History

British Transport Police History Society
15–17 Tavistock Place
London WC1 9SY

Garda Siochana Museum and Archives
The Records Tower
Dublin Castle
Dublin 2

The Glasgow Police Museum
68 St Andrews Square
Glasgow G1 5PR

The Hampshire Constabulary History Society
Southern Support and Training Headquarters
Victoria House
Netley
Hampshire

Imperial War Museum
Lambeth Road
London SE1 6HZ

The Metropolitan Police
MPS Records Management Branch
Empress State Building
Lille Road
London SW6 1TR

National Police Library
Centrex
Bramshill
Hook
Hampshire RG27 OJW

North Eastern Police History Society
Brinkburn Cottage
28 Brinkburn High Street
Barnes
Sunderland SR4 7RG

The Police History Society
Secretary
64 Nore Marsh Road
Wootton Bassett
Wiltshire SN4 8BH

Police Officers Roll of Honour Trust
PO Box 999
Preston PR4 5WW

Research into Family and Police History
52 Symons Avenue
Eastwood
Leigh on Sea
Essex SS9 5QE

Ripon Prison and Police Museum
St Marygate
Ripon

Surrey Police Museum
Mount Browne
Sandy Lane
Guildford
Surrey GU3 1 HG

Thames Valley Police Museum
Sulhamstead
Nr Reading
Berkshire RG7 4 DX

West Midlands Police Museum
Sparkhill Police Station
Stratford Road
Sparkhill
Birmingham
West Midlands B11 4EA

Journals

The Editor
Journal of the Police History Society
Pinewell Heights
Tilford Road
Hindhead
Surrey GU26 6SQ

Police Review: www.policereview.com

Family History Societies

Obviously, there are hundreds of these now, but this is a list of some main ones; clearly, a very productive first move in this context is to approach a society near you and perhaps find a member who has already done some police ancestor research.

The national organisations are:

The Association of Genealogists and Researchers in Archives (AGRA). This contains a resource of various specialist archivists who may help with queries. They are at agra.org.uk/page2 html

The Families in British India Society
This group will offer help in finding information on ancestors living in British India from about 1600. They are at: ffhs.org.uk

Jewish Genealogical Society of Great Britain
They can link to and give details of special interest groups who meet periodically with family history themes. They are at: jgsgb.org.uk

Railway Ancestors
Clearly this is a very useful point of contact with reference to transport police. They are at: railwayancestors.fsnet.co.uk

English Societies

British Record Society: britishrecordsociety.org.uk
Devon Family History Society (produces a journal and CDs of members' research): Devonfhs.org.uk
Hampshire Genealogical Society: hgs.online.org.uk
North West Kent Family History Society: nwkfhs.org.uk
Yorkshire Family History (linked to the long-established Yorkshire Archaeological Society): yorkshireroots.org.uk

Welsh Societies

Association of Family History Societies of Wales: fhswales.info
Glamorgan Family History Society: glamfhs.org
Monmouthshire Family History Society: gwentfhs.info
Pembrokeshire Family History Society: dyfedfhs.org.uk

Irish Societies

Genealogical Society of Ireland: familyhistory.ie
North of Ireland Family History Society: nifhs.org/society
The Irish Genealogical Research Society: igrsoc.org

Scottish Societies

Scottish Association of Family History Societies: safhs.org.uk
The Scottish Genealogy Society: scotsgenealogy.com

CONCLUSIONS

Recently the organisation Ingentaconnect featured an item on its website concerning the preservation of Metropolitan Police Service Records under the Greater London Authority. Ingentaconnect is a source for a range of citation data on over twenty million articles in journals and online. They focused on something of an issue with police historians: the fragmentary nature of police service records, an aspect that has been emphasised throughout this book.

Author A. Brown, in the *Records Management Journal* vol. 11, no. 1 (2001) addressed this question. He argued that the Greater London Authority Act of 1999, which made the Metropolitan Police Service records different in status from 'public records', will make the Authority, not the police force, responsible for the preservation of historical material, and so the fragmentation is even more likely to happen. Brown's article makes very clear the difficulties facing the police family historian today and in the future, following a research trajectory that sometimes feels like a form of historical 'snakes and ladders'. I hope that this book has made that tortuous path to the location of records a little easier, and that my various resources, from central material to fringe sources, will help the police family researcher open up some new lines of enquiry. In compiling these guidelines I too have learned just how difficult this version of family history is. The smaller constabularies in particular present the toughest challenge, and the tendency of historical research to require an element of 'detective footwork' is at its most apparent there.

What conclusions may we draw from this situation, in which so much determined paperwork (and footwork) has to be done in order for any headway to be made in tracing the constable on the beat in some small force long ago? The following is a summary of some possible examples and the resources available.

The most substantial records are for a prominent member of a force: a person who has perhaps been involved in events of national importance, or has achieved local prominence for sport and leisure activities, while even the most humble constable is likely to be mentioned in the everyday practice of recording crimes and criminals in the log books and charge books.

Then there are the researches that begin well with an opening from the internet listings such as Access to Archives, but peter out into a simple list of basic facts or perhaps a career profile.

Finally, determined enquiries may elicit random and scattered details from across the spectrum of newspaper material to be found in The Times Digital Archives or Nineteenth-Century British Newspapers Online.

In exceptional cases, the existence of photographs, medals and citations add a wonderful richness for the historian. Of course, the plain fact in most cases is that the majority of police work was regular routine surveillance and street presence, with the average constable being a known part of the locality. Why would any literature and documentation need to be created with regard to that work? For instance, a typical scenario of urban police work in late Victorian England might be the kind of profile of local crime reflected in the Dewsbury court records for 1888–1889. In the month of January that year the predominant offences were: drunk and disorderly conduct, vagrancy, bastardy, offences by pedlars, cruelty to animals and various types of assault. In 1889 there was a first sitting in a new courtroom. The senior police officer present was not named but was almost certainly William Airton, listed in the 1889 *Kelly's Directory* as Superintendent of the West Riding Police, but even that fact has to be inferred by the historian. In 1909 there was another assault on a police officer but all we have on record is: 'George Walton Ellis (Mirfield 25 Jan. Assault on police, fine £1.00, costs 4s. 1 month in custody.'

Moreover, even the time taken to locate the stories behind the more serious offences may not be rewarded by the gleaning of information about the constable concerned. It has to be said that all this is completely understandable when we reflect on the social history of police work and look at how the constable was defined in the job description. An instruction book for 1900 defines 'general conduct' in this way:

It must be understood that the maintenance of discipline, the obedience of all commands from superior officers and the diligent discharge of all duties, are the foundations of the efficiency of the force, and secure the greatest possible degree of well-being, comfort and contentment for every member of it. Young constables will, no doubt, at first find their duties rather trying, but the Chief Constable hopes that they will do their best and remember that the Police Service is no more difficult than any other honourable work . . .

When constables left the force, if all had gone well, they were given a certificate of conduct: 'Every man is entitled to a certificate showing his rank and period of service and the reason for leaving the force . . .'. Once again, this leads to details about records of service in such items as chief constables' books and occurrence books in general.

All this tells the historian that the key trend in police work has been effacement: the average constable fades into the background in the majority of narratives concerning crime. It is this tendency in police history that has resulted in the 'paperchase' that is police ancestry research today.

This may all sound rather discouraging, but as Sally Nex wrote in a recent article on police ancestry in *Family History Monthly*: 'The first police forces in the 13th century were little more than one watchman doing the rounds in his village. They were quite well organised: the names of the watchmen and the exact route of their beat were recorded street by street – along with rates of pay, equipment and duties.' In other words, there was meticulous documentation from the beginning, so where these do survive, then there is cause for optimism for the historian in the family.

Finally, as another note of encouragement, one 'doorstep' source of access to police history in the media is the local newspaper index in the local studies library. In one of the nearest libraries to me, at Hull, we have items such as these:

Affray: between Hull police and seamen of the *Cornwallis*

Anniversary: 30th anniversary Hull Police Force

Chief Constable: Death of Andrew McManus, Chief Constable of Hull

Death at Lincoln 8 July, aged 51, John Mason, chief constable. Deceased was formerly a compositor in the *Advertiser* office and was subsequently employed on the *Watchman*. For the last 17 years he had sustained several public offices in Lincoln, and as a mark of the esteem in which he was held, upwards of 3,000 persons attended the sad rites paid to his remains.

Hull Police: Inspection

Police station houses: Specific mention of Jarratt Street police station, where there was a child fatality.

All these references have catalogue index numbers, and it may be seen from this that a good index often has the beginnings of a biographical source, as for Lincoln's Chief Constable John Mason. Therefore, whether the source is a well established and structured piece of documentation, or whether it is merely a scrap of information in a local paper, the fact is that all of these can be put together to form the narrative of your ancestor, and the pleasure is in the sheer dogged detective work of digging out that individual story from the mass of social history and paperwork generated by the force in question.

As with all research, what will almost always happen is the 'serendipity factor' – when a piece of information gleaned from the process of research will lead the historian to something of major interest, even though it may not have been the research brief of that particular day's work.

APPENDIX I

REGIONAL CRIME HISTORY

A s was mentioned with reference to the availability of lists of officers mentioned in newspaper reports, it has to be added that there is another way to find out fairly quickly if your police ancestor was involved in a crime story. This does not necessarily mean that he or she was part of the hunt for a mass murderer or that the name of the ancestor is going to appear in major works of true crime. But a quick check in the index of a series book from one of the specialist regional or local crime casebooks may reveal your officer featuring in a story.

There are five on-going series from three different publishers currently being printed regularly, and these volumes are gradually covering most of the cities and towns of Britain and Ireland. The main series are: 'Foul Deeds and Suspicious Deaths' (Wharncliffe/Pen & Sword Publishers); the 'County Murders' series (Countryside Books); the 'Murder and Crime In . . . ' series (Tempus); 'County Murders' (Tempus) and 'Hanging Chronicles' (Tempus). A typical description of what may be found in these books is given in this summary of *Cumbria Murders* by Paul Heslop:

> *Cumbria Murders* brings together numerous murderous tales that not only shocked the county but also made headlines throughout the country . . . Paul Heslop was a policeman for over thirty years, mostly as a detective. His experience and understanding of the criminal justice system give authority to his unbiased assessment and analysis of the cases . . .

In the Wharncliffe 'Foul Deeds and Suspicious Deaths' series all categories of crime are covered, so there is more likelihood that ordinary police constables will have been caught up in the narrative of a particular offence; more importantly, perhaps, the constable concerned would often be someone who knew and lived in the community in which the crime occurred. As an example, a search through the index for my own volume on Halifax (2004) finds twelve officers of various ranks embroiled in the action, as were these two men in a murder case from 1909: 'Two sergeants, Ramsden and Whitaker, searched Thwaites's home but found no knife. They found a puppy, a bed recently slept in, and on the table, a long signed confession from the young man who worked as a painter and paper-hanger at Robinson's . . .'.

As an example of how a story like this can be amplified as time goes on, not only was the crime featured in my book, but it also emerged again in a family history magazine article when someone discovered the murder in their work on their own family history.

Keith Henson's volume on York in the same series has a feature on 'A Policeman's Lot', which gives a fine example of how regional crime books can often supply the kind of social history in which police work was embedded. Some of the experiences recorded in that chapter give excellent illustrations of the kinds of story in which your ancestor may have been involved. At the most violent end of the spectrum of police work we have Constable Carter, who was 'set upon by four men and given a severe beating', leaving him 'a dreadful picture of brutality'. The men were never identified and no motive was given, 'other than he was a policeman', Henson writes. Then we have a full account of PC Cowton, who policed the rough area of the Bedern. Cowton was formerly an inmate of the workhouse, but joined the constabulary in 1852 and lived in the Bedern community with his wife and six children. Henson described one of his fairly regular confrontations in this way:

> Cowton was called at 1 a.m. to break up an argument that had turned violent. He found the whole neighbourhood in the alley, but alone he entered the affray and tried to disperse it. Tempers flared and one man threatened Cowton's life. Luckily, another policeman arrived and the two of them chased who they believed were the ringleaders . . .

It may be seen from these examples that a little time spent with volumes of regional crime casebooks may well be something that opens up the most memorable moment of an ancestor's police career. After all, the 'foul deeds' of the books include exactly the kinds of offence recorded in the police charge books, the most common in the mid-Victorian years being vagrancy, poaching, drunkenness, assault, larceny, cruelty to animals and threatening behaviour. But where a simple line in the listings of a charge book may include the officer's name, the fuller account in a casebook gives you the fruits of the research already done by the crime historian.

As these volumes are usually presented in chronological order, they also give the researcher a useful picture of the development of police work in the city or town the ancestor worked in, and the usual photographs add even more detail, bringing to life the working conditions of the officer's daily life.

Appendix II

A GUIDE TO
THE ARCHIVES OF THE
POLICE FORCES

Materials and Professional Context

Further to the general remarks given in Chapter 2, the following is a summary of the materials held in county archives from two constabularies: the Lincolnshire Constabulary held at Lincolnshire Archives and the East Riding Constabulary held at East Riding Archives, Beverley.

The Lincolnshire material includes archives from Boston Borough Police and Lincoln City Police. The lists of categories and items provide the historian with a fairly typical profile of what is likely to be found in any of the other force archives in the Police History Society/Open University database. For instance, the categories of items are: station journals, information on personnel, minutes and reports from Standing Joint Committees and Watch Committees, a miscellaneous group, sections on both world wars, Civil Defence sources and finally, material from the Boston and Lincoln forces. All this material is listed and summarised in chronological order, so the researcher in the archives will benefit from reading through them in that order, taking in the pointers towards the social history before deciding what is likely to be useful. But clearly the first point of interest is in the personnel category. Here, there are the registers of the force, covering recruitment and constables for the period 1857–1939, and including the Boston Division.

There is also a defaulters book and a register of complaints against constables.

For the years 1884–1899 the historian will begin by noting that the county has always been split into the areas known as Holland, Lindsey and Kesteven, and so that is the first entry into the location of the ancestor's force. Fortunately for Lincolnshire enquiries, there is also a collection of pay books, and these cover the years 1884–1899 for both Holland and Kesteven.

Moving forward into the twentieth century, the material includes approval registers for Cleethorpes, Gainsborough, Spalding and Stamford, and so there would be little trouble in locating the activities of the ancestor if he was part of any initiative linked to promotions that went before the chief constable. However, the chief constable's recommendations for promotion were not the only ones: for the period 1938–1940 commendations were also given by people outside the constabulary in question, presumably related to wartime activity.

The Watch and Standing Joint Committee collection comprises: Quarter Sessions orders for Holland; reports by chief constables to justices in Holland, Lindsey and Kesteven; Standing Joint Committee materials for all three areas covering the years 1902–1937, and the Police Committee minutes for 1937–1964. Added to that, we also have specific responsibilities logged by such items as minutes of the Police Houses committee and the Emergency Sub-Committee.

When you consider the kind of society reflected in the charge books of late Victorian and Edwardian England, it comes as no surprise to see the wealth of material that is contained in the miscellaneous material, and to note what this kind of source tells us about policing in those years. The material covering the years 1867 to 1931 includes: police manuals, a Contagious Diseases Handbook, a report on Police Systems in Urban Districts, fingerprint clues, details of the Metropolitan Police Training School syllabus, notes on traffic signals, Contagious Diseases of Animals, and materials on poachers and preserves. Of course, every historian in this context will need to be aware of the particular circumstances of the region in question in order to understand the ancestor's place in that work and community; so, for instance, the Lincolnshire archive has items on the Lincolnshire floods, along with chief constables' reports.

Of course, the two world wars play a part in these police archives in all parts of the land. In Lincolnshire, naturally, the First World War meant that there were spy networks at the docks in Grimsby and at

Boston, and the possibility of an enemy invasion was a part of the scene as well. Therefore the materials include papers regarding the invasion, War Committee minutes and a category titled 'Civil disturbances and the employment of the military'. In the 1914–1918 period, the various orders and circulars related to such items as duties at docks, checking on aliens and monitoring movements and transport across the 'patch'. This was certainly not an over-reaction; these were the early years of MI5 and the intervention by security forces (police and military) into private mail, and by these means some spies were actually found and arrested.

In the Second World War, of course, Lincolnshire, in common with everywhere else, suffered air raids that brought a new dimension to the policing routine. This is reflected in the archives, with listings of supplies and issues registers, daily situation reports, bomb damage reports, printed pamphlets for Civil Defence, Home Security Circulars, air raid precaution materials and Civil Defence training bulletins. In memoirs such as Bert Fryer's (discussed previously) we have an insight into the circumstances of ordinary police work in rural Lincolnshire in wartime. In *Recollections of a Country Copper* (p. 81), Fryer wrote:

> Whilst on the subject of the Luftwaffe I recall the occasion when I heard my first bomb explode. My duty for that day was 4–7 pm and 11 to 5 am and my first Conference Point on the 11–5 shift was to be at twelve midnight at a public house then known as the Plankhook and Shovel on Holbeach Bank . . . As I was about to go on duty at eleven I received a message . . . My Special Constable sergeant, who was a first war soldier, was with me and we went down together. Whilst we were there standing on the sea bank we could hear enemy planes overhead and at just about midnight the noise of a heavy thud came from the direction of Holbeach . . .

Fryer later found out that the bomb had landed just 50 yards from where he would have been at midnight had he not been called to the beach.

The records often have notes relating to the harsh reality of police work in the wars, but these are not as readable as Fryer's memoir. Nevertheless, police had to be aware of air raid wardens' bulletins and be trained to handle fires, check house damage and of course be fully briefed on what to do if the enemy invaded. Many of the archive materials will have a few sentences giving a more human, personal side of events, rather than just the bare facts. Of course, the material extends into the 1960s and so the later archives include such things as 'radio-active fallout information', reports on the 'Hydrogen Bomb' and a 'Counter Sabotage Handbook'.

It is when we come to the material on the Boston Borough force and on the Lincoln City Police that the really important family history material is found. The Boston Borough Police existed from 1836 to 1947, and the family historian will find here the Watch Committee minute books for 1873–1903, so there will be names and payments recorded, along with notes on the police establishment, travelling to court, police houses and so on. Rather more colourful and certainly informative are the reports in the disciplinary report book for 1920–1947.

Lincolnshire Archives also holds material on the Grantham Borough force, which was in existence for the same period as the Boston constabulary. Here we have a register of complaints against police officers for 1866–1919 and a criminals identity book for 1872–1930. Lincoln City Police was one of the very first founded in England, in 1829, and it only ceased to exist in 1967. The archives have a police register for 1857–1901, a journal and standing orders. Particularly interesting is CID material for the years 1902–1906.

The material for the East Riding Constabulary (1857–1968) covers similar ground, but there are particularly unusual and interesting items for the family historian, notably (for the early period) a report on the Daily State of the Force 1904–1914 and the Anti Gas Training Receipt Book, which gives names. The heart of the collection has to be the beat books – in 33 volumes – for the years after 1928, and there are also occurrence books for the war years. The most intriguing and surely very rare item is listed as 'Police note books 31 volumes'.

For the Hull City Police (1836–1974), also at Beverley, we have the personnel register for 1860 to 1919 and a register for personnel rewards and commendations 1860–1920, along with memos from the chief constable. (For this force, see also the item by Roger Swift in the Bibliography, as his Borthwick paper covers the early years of the Hull City Police.)

It may be seen from this that the listings on this central database have very helpful indications about what is held where, and what the potential usefulness (or otherwise) for the family historian is likely to be. As already stated, the recommended approach in using these materials is to start with the mere listings of service and then move on, using this process:

1. Begin with notes on the record of service, warrant number and other basic facts.

2. Using the timespan now acquired, look in the material relating to the second level, such as commendations, promotions, etc.

3. Progress to the social context, study the local history and note any important social factors like mass immigration in the area or new industries, political agitation and so on.

4. Look in wider sources for details of these and use the indices of police officers in newspapers as well as the regional crime studies discussed above.

All this may seem like an arduous and largely thankless task, but actually it is pure detective work. After all, the activity at the heart of this book is one of dredging a 'life' from the silt and mud of the past, but the satisfaction of reclaiming a life in this sense is a great reward for the investment of time and brainwork involved. As with real detective work, the principal virtues required are patience and sheer dogged persistence. Also, as with all historical research and writing, one of the delights in the work is in assembling the fragments of the past life into a full picture, and so feeling the satisfaction of having attained something genuinely new.

Appendix III

USE OF PRE-VICTORIAN ANCILLARY SOURCES

As indicated in the introductory historical survey, gaining access to documentary sources for police history before the 1829 Act and the main Victorian developments is often difficult. Most of the categories of document are concerned with the social history and routine of police work, but occasionally they offer some valuable materials. The varieties of miscellaneous source documents tend to come under these headings:

Documents on the police establishment

Watch Committee materials

Local constables' reports

Research into the actual physical side of policing is best pursued by reference to the use and construction of lock-ups, and a short account of police property in Northallerton will show the chequered history of these places. The North Riding Constabulary was formed on 14 October 1856 and the first office of the Chief Constable was built in East Street. This was after a grant of land made in 1849 'for the appointment and payment of parish constables'. Then in 1857 the force was split into three divisions.

By 1880 a new headquarters had been built near Northallerton prison, but after only twenty-seven years this was found to be inadequate to meet the changing needs, and so new plans were made for the construction of a new headquarters near County Hall in the town. After the

Edwardian period the former lock-up and headquarters were used by the council for storage, and after the Second World War the old head-quarters were used as the base for the County Fire Brigade until 1968, when yet another police headquarters were built.

Tracing this history helps to make sense of the archives relating to the ancestor's daily work, particularly when there is material on the beat, as in the report from the Richmond Watch Committee referred to in Chapter 2, in which a researcher has found details of the exact itinerary of the constable's beat in 1783, such as 'At General Fitzwilliam's to go round the green at the back of the playhouse and into the Old Court, back to his box.' If we put together the details of a beat, the location of the lock-ups and station, and then the local maps available, we can build a very clear picture of what the ancestor's daily work would have been like in preserving the peace.

He also had to report of course, and in Worcester County Record Office (WRO I 595) we have a typical example from 1635:

Presentment of Edward Barry, Constable of Mumble, taken by William Boraston one of the High Constables of the Hundred of Dodingtree as followeth. For recusants, Jesuits, seminaries or any of that profession I know not of any in our liberties [an area located outside a borough]. There are two alehouses which are licensed to keep true assize of bread and beer and lodging for man and for horse and the necessaries according to my true believing. Our high-ways are in good repair. I have apprehended and punished several persons by whipping and taking fines, my last being our monthly meeting of our Justices. We have no common swearers, drunkards or anything like idle persons or anything else belonging to my office at this time fitting to present otherwise.

Appendix IV

ACADEMIC MONOGRAPHS AND JOURNALS

The local and family historian could be forgiven for overlooking this fascinating source. This is because the material is usually tucked away in learned journals in university libraries, but the kind of monographs listed in the Bibliography contain a wealth of material. Peter Bramham's study of the Keighley constabulary typifies this usefulness.

Bramham set about answering the question: 'How did citizens manage before the mid-nineteenth century, when there were no professional police forces at all?' He then delved into the issues relevant to his particular community: 'Why was Keighley slow to develop into a municipal authority with an efficient autonomous police force enforcing law and order within the framework of borough status?' Bramham's enquiry later focused on the life and work of a constable known as 'Pie' Leach, whose diary has survived and covers the years 1848 to 1853.

The politics of the place actually brings out names and incidents, as in the effects of outside interference with the work of the Watch Committee; one of their watchmen, John Broderick, was sacked by means of the magistrates exerting pressure on the superintendent. The Watch Committee then set up an enquiry into the sacking. When an officer named Kershaw applied for promotion, the Committee wrote: 'This Board wishes to record its cordial recognition of the very valuable services rendered to it, and to the inhabitants of Keighley at large by Mr

Kershaw . . . the Board recommends him as an officer fully competent to perform the duties of Superintendent of Police.'

It may be seen from this that monographs often do much of the hard work at the archives for the family historian; it is then merely a case of locating them, and the way to do this is to use the Bibliography of British Police History which is found at: http://www.open.ac.uk/Arts/ policebiblio/.

Appendix V

CONTEMPORARY BIOGRAPHY

If one needs biographical information on police officers of high status, then there are various categories of contemporary biography for the period *c.* 1780–1900 in particular, often produced for the new and expanding middle-class readership of the time. From the mid-eighteenth century onwards London booksellers (who were also publishers) saw the growing market for such works. Hack writers would be commissioned to produce biographies of eminent persons, including people in the criminal justice system. Into the Victorian period the new magazines expanded this interest still further, as in the case study I have included on the Thames Police from the *Strand* magazine.

As early as 1820 the *Biographical Magazine* offered 'portraits of eminent and ingenious persons' (published by Effingham Wilson in 1820). By the end of the century (1894) we have *Haydn's Book of Dignitaries*, published by W.H. Allen. Such works provide more than the standard almanacs, and together with the proliferation of popular weekend and leisure magazines, they provide an extra dimension to police history. A typical entry would be someone like Patrick Colquhoun or the Commissioners of the Metropolitan and City Police forces, but the true value of the pieces is in the provision they have for summarising the work and professional duties of the men concerned.

In the magazines the interest was often primarily documentary, as can be seen in the account of the Thames Police, in which (like Charles Dickens with the new detective force after 1842) the interest was the fascination with the 'alternative city' of night-time London. But often the journals of the Victorian period provide stories of crime and its social background in reasonable depth, and the officers come along with those stories. Dickens himself ran a publication called the *Household Narrative* to supplement his *Household Words,* and throughout the 1850s this journal provided regional as well as metropolitan crime summaries. All are useful sources for the family historian.

INDEX